Peter's
BAKING PARTY

Peter's
BAKING PARTY

Fun & Tasty Recipes for Future Baking Stars!

PETER SAWKINS

BLACK & WHITE PUBLISHING

First published in the UK in 2022 by
Black & White Publishing Ltd
Nautical House, 104 Commercial Street, Edinburgh, EH6 6NF

A division of Bonnier Books UK
4th Floor, Victoria House, Bloomsbury Square, London, WC1B 4DA
Owned by Bonnier Books
Sveavägen 56, Stockholm, Sweden

All photography by Susie Lowe

A CIP catalogue record for this book is available from the British Library.

ISBN: 978 1 78530 414 9

1 3 5 7 9 10 8 6 4 2

Design by Black & White Publishing
Printed and bound in Great Britain by Bell & Bain Ltd, Glasgow

www.blackandwhitepublishing.com

This book is dedicated to my
Auntie Rachel and Mum.

For my mum's inspiration to me
in the kitchen as a young child and
my auntie's inspiration to me and
thousands of children in her
years as a teacher.

CONTENTS

WELCOME TO MY BAKING PARTY!

I'm Peter, and I love baking! I have baked for as long as I can remember. It started with making the simplest recipes with my mum, and then from the age of twelve I got completely hooked. I tried all the techniques I saw on TV and read in books, and learned as much about baking as possible. Baking is special to me, and I find it incredibly fun and exciting. I want to share this excitement with you through this book.

The goal of this book and every recipe inside is to inspire you to get baking. I want you to try baking because it helps us develop creativity, resilience, numeracy and literacy skills, kitchen skills, independence, teamwork, self-confidence and more, without even realising it. When you bake, it's just about having fun and sharing your creations with the people you love. You don't even realise the skills and attributes you're developing, and that's the magic of baking.

I have developed these recipes to be fun and exciting, thinking about what I used to and still love to bake. But I also talked to school children to hear what they wanted to see. I love every recipe here, and I hope you will love them too. Many of them are very simple, perfect whether you have zero kitchen experience or years of it.

However, I want you to know that this isn't just a basic baking book: there is proper baking here. Some of the most difficult recipes are quite challenging and you will need some practice to build up the skills for them. It was important for me to put in these challenging bakes. My auntie is a primary school teacher, and she told me 'You should never underestimate what a child can do'. If you are passionate about something and apply yourself to it, you can do amazing things, maybe even things that you thought weren't possible when you first picked up something new. So, no matter what age you are or how much prior experience you have, you can use this book for a fun activity and bake for the odd bake sale. Or, if you become hugely passionate about baking, you can work through the difficulty levels of the book, stretch yourself and develop into a star baker.

Thanks for coming to my party. I hope you have a blast!

Peter

WHY WE BAKE

There are many reasons why I love to 'bake and it is so important to me. This is why I want you to get excited and start in the kitchen. Baking is pure fun, but the experience can be even more amazing when we take time to reflect on why we bake and why baking can be special . . .

TO SPEND TIME WITH LOVED ONES

To say thank you to friends and family

To explore new flavours and foods

To challenge yourself TO HAVE FUN!

TO CELEBRATE BIG EVENTS

To eat delicious bakes!

TO MAKE OTHERS HAPPY

TO IMPROVE OUR READING AND NUMBER SKILLS

To develop kitchen skills

To explore our imagination and creativity

HOW TO USE THIS BOOK

BEFORE THE RECIPES, YOU WILL FIND SOME EXTRA NOTES ABOUT BAKING:

BASIC TECHNIQUES

These are fuller explanations of some basic and very common baking techniques. You will be a great baker if you can understand and master these techniques.

INGREDIENTS

This is a list of the most common baking ingredients that are great to have in your store cupboards.

EQUIPMENT

This is a list of the equipment you will need to bake all the recipes in this book.

Oven temperatures

I use a fan-assisted, electric oven. If you are using a conventional electric oven, add 10°C to the temperature stated. I have also listed the temperatures in Fahrenheit for conventional ovens

THE RECIPE PAGES ARE ALL LAID OUT WITH THIS INFORMATION ON THE PAGE:

Recipe key

QUANTITY

Telling you roughly how many portions this recipe will produce.

TIME REQUIRED

How long this recipe will take to bake with hands-on prep, baking and proving. This is an estimation, so depending on how experienced you are in the kitchen, the time it takes you might vary.

BAKING CHALLENGE

This is a difficulty rating for the bake out of 5. Level 1 bakes are super simple, ideal for first-time bakers or when you need to make a fail-safe bake. Level 5 bakes are some of the toughest bakes I would make when I was thirteen or fourteen years

old. If you can bake the level 5 bakes in this book, I think you have the skills to tackle virtually any bake you want to attempt. I hope there is a good range of ability levels in this book, and you can progress through the levels as you get more practised in the kitchen.

GF/GFO

If a recipe has 'GF' in the key, it is gluten-free. If the recipe has 'GFO' in the key, there is a gluten-free option for the bake, which will be explained in a box on the recipe page. You can find a list of all the gluten-free recipes at the back of the book.

INGREDIENTS LIST

Check you have all the ingredients you will need before starting the bake.

METHOD

I have tried to give you lots of detail in the methods whilst keeping them simple to follow. If you don't understand what something means or how to do a technique, either look to the 'Basic Techniques' section of this book (page 15) or search for the technique on YouTube. You can find loads of great videos explaining baking techniques online.

'Make this gluten-free'

This box will tell you the ingredient and technique changes you need to make a 'GFO' recipe gluten-free.

'Bake it your own'

This box will give ideas for how you can make small changes to the ingredients or techniques to turn the basic recipe into something new.

BEFORE YOU BAKE CHECKLIST

Sometimes we bake for specific people and occasions, sometimes we just bake for ourselves, but there is always a story and connection behind everything we bake. I have designed this checklist to go through before you bake to make sure everything you bake will be really special:

1. WHO AM I BAKING FOR?

Is it a friend, your family, teacher or coach, or maybe just yourself?

2. WHY AM I BAKING FOR THEM?

Could it be to say thank you, celebrate their birthday or a special occasion, cheer them up after a tough time, just for a fun activity, or something else?

3. ASK YOUR GROWN-UP

Make sure your grown-up is happy with you baking today and can be on hand if you need some help during the bake.

4. WHAT ARE THEIR FAVOURITE FLAVOURS OR BAKES?

Try to think of any conversations you have had with them and see if you can remember any of their favourites. People are so thankful when you remember their favourites, and it shows a lot of care and attention from you.

5. HOW MUCH TIME DO I HAVE?

Look at the time required and difficulty ratings in the key at the top of the recipe pages. Make sure you have enough time to make the bake without rushing.

6. DO I HAVE THE INGREDIENTS AND EQUIPMENT?

Read through the ingredients list and method. If you don't have what you need for that recipe, you can either plan to make a couple of changes or just pick a different recipe today and come back to that one later.

7. GET BAKING AND HAVE FUN!!!!

WHAT TO DO IF IT ALL GOES WRONG?!

I have been baking for over fifteen years, and I still make mistakes in the kitchen. Mistakes happen less and less as you practise more, but even the most experienced bakers will still slip up every once in a while.

A baking fail can be really annoying and sometimes upsetting, but they can also be great opportunities to learn and create. If a cake sinks or pastry falls apart, you can try to figure out why and how this happened so it doesn't happen again. Research your problem online or read the notes in this book to find an answer. In doing this, you become more knowledgeable about baking and can transfer this knowledge into different areas of baking as well.

Baking fails are also a fantastic time to use your creativity. If your bake hasn't turned out how you wanted, take a moment to think about what you can do to turn this bake into something beautiful and delicious to serve up. Maybe you break it up into small pieces and mix it through ice cream. Maybe you cover up cracks with extra decorations or icing. Maybe you rename a wonky cake to make people think it was meant to be leaning. If you really can't think of anything, my go-to is to cover it in custard. Everything tastes great covered in custard. Even if you think the bake has gone terribly wrong, it will probably still taste great.

Baking should be pure fun, not stressful and worrying. When things go wrong, try to learn from it. Create something new with what you have, and remember this line from my dad, who would remind me of this if I ever started to worry about my baking whilst on Bake-Off: 'It's only cake.' Cake is a special thing, but if it goes wrong, it's really not a problem worth worrying about.

BAKING NOTES

Hygiene and Safety

Always make sure you check with your grown-up before starting to bake. If you have questions whilst baking, ask for some help. When we first start baking, we all need a lot of help, but as we bake more and get used to the process, we can start to do more by ourselves.

HYGIENE

- ☆ Before baking, always wash your hands thoroughly with soap and warm water for 20 seconds.

- ☆ Frequently wash your hands whilst baking, especially if they get covered in some ingredients or after handling raw meat.

- ☆ Wipe your surfaces with surface cleaner followed by water before baking.

KEEP CLEAN

- ☆ Tidy up as you go when baking. This keeps your worktop clear and helps you stay organised and bake better whilst staying hygienic.

- ☆ I like to wash my dishes whenever I have a couple of minutes waiting whilst baking. This means I never have a giant pile of dishes to clean at the end of a bake, and I can tackle it a couple of minutes at a time.

BE PREPARED

- ☆ Before baking, make sure you have all the ingredients and equipment you need close by.

- ☆ Read through the full recipe before starting, so you know what you will have to do later on.

SAFETY

Hot things

- ☆ Take care when dealing with anything hot in the kitchen, including the oven, the hob and any hot tins or pans.

- ☆ Use oven gloves whenever moving something in or out of the oven.

- ☆ If you burn yourself, quickly move to the sink and run the burn under cool water for a few minutes.

- ☆ Tell a grown-up if you have hurt yourself so they can help you.

Sharp things

- ☆ When dealing with knives, cutters or graters, keep your fingers far away from the sharp side of the equipment at all times.

- ☆ Take your time when using sharp knives and get some supervision. It is important to learn how to use sharp knives and to become confident using them.

- ☆ Never place sharp items into a washing-up basin full of water. You always need to see the blades so no one accidentally cuts their hands on them.

- ☆ If you do hurt yourself, tell a grown-up as soon as possible.

Ingredients

BUTTER

I use unsalted butter in my recipes and add some salt to most recipes. If you only have salted butter, you can use this and leave out any extra salt.

When making cakes or other bakes that require you to cream butter, try to leave it out at room temperature for a couple of hours before baking, so it is softened.

EGGS

I typically use large British eggs (extra large US eggs) when making my recipes, but you should be fine to use any size of eggs for these recipes. If possible, it is best to use eggs at room temperature when baking.

MILK

When I call for milk in recipes, you can use any milk you like, from cow's milk to any milk alternative like oat or almond milk.

SUGAR

Caster sugar

Caster sugar is your standard sugar for baking. If you don't have caster sugar available, you can use granulated sugar.

Brown sugar

Brown sugar has molasses in it, which makes it darker in colour. This brings a caramel-like flavour and chewy texture to bakes.

Icing sugar (confectioner's sugar)

Icing sugar, also called confectioner's sugar, is a very finely ground sugar mixed with a bit of starch. This makes it perfect for dusting over finished bakes and mixing into icings.

CREAM

I always bake with double cream (heavy cream) rather than single cream. Double cream has more fat than single cream and can be whipped into a firm shape. You can substitute this for whipping cream.

I often like to use longer-life double cream, so there is always some cream handy in my fridge if I need to whip up a quick cake. In addition, the brand of long-life cream in the UK called Elmlea can't be overwhipped unlike double cream. This is a helpful note to remember.

SALT

Salt lifts the flavour of bakes. The finished product won't taste salty with the quantity I have in these sweet recipes. However, it makes the bake taste better on the whole.

YEAST

Yeast is added to bread to make it rise. I always use fast-action dried yeast which comes in small tins or sachets and can be found next to flour in supermarkets.

FLOUR

These are the three main types of flour in this book:

Plain (all-purpose)

Plain flour is typically used to make bakes that need to stay crumbly or soft, like biscuits, pastry and cookies.

Self-raising (self-rising)

Self-raising flour is plain flour with baking powder added to help bakes like cakes and soda bread rise. You can buy ready-made self-raising flour or make your own by adding 1 teaspoon of baking powder per 100g (3½oz) of plain flour.

Strong bread flour

Strong bread flour contains more protein than plain flour, which creates more gluten formation, leading to chewier, springier bakes. This is why this flour is used for making bread.

LEAVENING AGENTS

Bicarbonate of soda (baking soda)

When bicarbonate of soda is mixed with an acidic liquid, it starts to bubble and makes the batter rise, making a bake with a lighter texture.

Baking powder

Baking powder is like bicarbonate of soda but starts working when mixed with any liquid. They do similar things, but you cannot substitute baking powder and bicarbonate of soda one for one.

GLUTEN-FREE

Gluten-free flour blends

I use ready-made gluten-free flour blends from the shop, which combine lots of different starches and grains to create flour without gluten. This book uses gluten-free plain and self-raising flour blends. My favourite brand of gluten-free flour in the UK is from a company called Doves Farm.

Xanthan gum

Xanthan gum is an interesting ingredient that thickens the mixtures it is added to and holds it together. This is useful to prevent gluten-free bakes from being too crumbly. You can find this in most free-from sections in supermarkets.

Psyllium husk powder

You can buy this specialist ingredient online or in health food stores. I buy mine from Amazon. You need psyllium husk powder in gluten-free bread to give it structure and help it rise.

Always check the ingredients

If you are making a gluten-free bake, check all of your ingredients for gluten before baking with them. Depending on the brand, some ingredients will or won't have gluten, e.g. chocolate, baking powder, and sprinkles.

Equipment

I have tried to write this book using as little equipment as possible. This list of equipment will allow you to make every recipe in this book and would make for a very well-equipped kitchen for baking. However, you don't need to get every tin at the start of your baking journey. Start with the basics, then you can build up equipment over time depending on how much you bake and what you like to bake.

- ☆ Electric hand mixer
- ☆ 2 x flat baking trays
- ☆ 2 x 18cm (7") round cake tins
- ☆ 1 x 900g (2lb) loaf tin
- ☆ 1 x 20cm (8") square cake tin
- ☆ 1 x 20cm (8") round loose-bottomed cake tin
- ☆ 1 x 23x33cm (9"x13") roasting tin

- ☆ 1 x 20cm (8") round loose-bottomed tart tin
- ☆ 1 x 12-hole muffin tray
- ☆ Balloon whisk
- ☆ Spatula
- ☆ Palette knife
- ☆ Rolling pin
- ☆ Sieve
- ☆ Mixing bowls
- ☆ Measuring spoons

- ☆ Measuring jug
- ☆ Digital weighing scales
- ☆ Piping bags
- ☆ Round cookie cutters
- ☆ Grater
- ☆ Knife
- ☆ Chopping boards
- ☆ Ruler

BASIC TECHNIQUES

Weighing ingredients

It is very important to weigh ingredients accurately to see consistent results. It is easiest to weigh ingredients accurately with an electric scale.

1. Place your bowl onto your scales. Press the button that says 'zero' or 'tare'. This will make the scale read '0g'.
2. Add an ingredient into the bowl until the scale reads the number you are looking for. Add ingredients gradually using a spoon to make sure you weigh an accurate amount.
3. Reset the scale to zero before weighing more ingredients into the same bowl.

Lining tins

It is important to line cake tins and baking trays to make sure your bakes don't get stuck. This is a quick guide of how to line the main types of tins and trays used in this book.

BAKING TRAY

1. Cut a sheet of baking paper the same size as the baking tray and lay this over the tray.

LOAF TIN

1. Use your hand to rub a thin layer of butter over all the surface inside the tin.
2. Cut a sheet of baking paper from a roll that is the same width as the base of the loaf tin but quite long.

3. Place this sheet of baking paper into the tin so it covers the base and wide sides of the tin and overhangs.
4. The overhang will be useful to help remove your cake from the tin later.

ROUND CAKE TIN

1. Use your hand to rub a thin layer of butter all over the surface inside the tin.

2. Cut a square of baking paper that is a little larger than the tin.

3. Fold this square in half, then half again the other way to make a smaller square.

4. Fold this square in half to create a triangle. Fold this triangle in half two more times in the same direction to make a very skinny triangle.

5. Lay the triangle over the tin, with the point over the centre of the tin. Cut the edge off the baking paper at the edge of the tin.

6. Unfold the baking paper triangle to reveal a circle. Fit this into the bottom of the cake tin.

SQUARE CAKE TIN

1. Use your hand to rub a thin layer of butter over all the surface inside the tin.

2. Cut a square of baking paper about the same size as the cake tin. Fit this into the bottom of the cake tin.

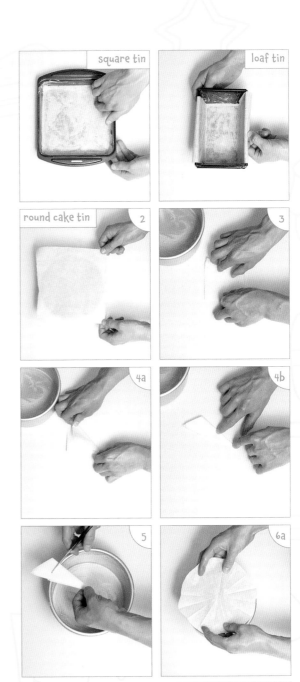

Creaming

Creaming is the process of beating butter and sugar together. This smooths out the butter, dissolves the sugar and adds air to the mixture, giving your finished bakes a lighter texture.

1. Make sure your butter is room temperature and soft. It should be easily spreadable. Try to take your butter out of the fridge a couple of hours before baking. If you need to soften butter quickly, chop it into small cubes and microwave on the defrost setting for 10-second bursts, stirring after each burst until the butter is spreadable.

2. Add the softened butter and sugar into a large mixing bowl. Beat at high speed with an electric whisk for about 5 minutes.

3. The butter and sugar will look crumbly at first, then will become smoother. Keep beating the butter until it looks very light and creamy, and is a lot less yellow than at the start. Be patient with this step. It's worth creaming for a long time when recommended in the recipe.

Rubbing in

This is combining flour and fat (butter) before adding liquid into the mix. This coats the flour with fat, which stops bakes from becoming tough. This is because the fat stops the flour from creating structures of gluten, which make bakes like bread springy and chewy.

1. Chop up your butter into small cubes. It can be room temperature or cold butter.
2. Coat the lumps of butter in flour and rub them between your fingertips to break them apart. As you rub the butter into the flour, lift your hands and let the flour and butter fall back into the bowl.
3. As the lumps of butter become smaller, gently shake the bowl. This will bring any large lumps of butter up to the top of the bowl. Try to break up these larger pieces.
4. You have finished rubbing in once you can't see any large lumps of butter, and it all looks like quite a fine crumbly texture.

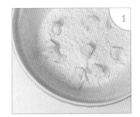

Folding

Many recipes in baking require us to whip eggs or cream, so we can trap lots of air in the mixture and make the bake light and airy. Folding is a technique of mixing ingredients to avoid losing the trapped air from the mix. I recommend you get a flexible spatula for folding.

1. Combine the two mixtures you want to fold together in a large bowl.
2. Pull the edge of the spatula through the middle of the mixture (sometimes called a cut), scrape the mixture from the bottom of the bowl and around the side and lift/fold it onto itself.
3. Turn the bowl 90 degrees (a quarter turn) and repeat the process of cutting the spatula through the middle of the bowl and scraping and folding the mixture onto itself.
4. Stop folding as soon as the mixture is combined and no longer streaky. If you continue folding, you will knock out the air from the mixture.

Kneading

Kneading is the process of pressing dough with your hands, so it becomes combined and smoother. Kneading a dough creates a protein network called gluten which makes the dough stretchy and springy. When kneading bread dough, you want lots of gluten, so you must knead it for a long time. When making biscuits or pastry, you don't want much gluten, so you want to knead it just until it comes together in a dough and no further.

1. Stir together your wet and dry ingredients until they come together into a dough and you can no longer see any liquid.

2. Tip this out onto a work surface and use your hands to squeeze the mixture together until it forms into one ball of dough.

3. Press down and away on one side of the dough with the heel of one of your hands whilst gently holding the dough in place with your other hand. The goal here is to stretch the dough.

4. Roll the stretched dough back on itself and turn it 90 degrees (a quarter turn).

5. Repeat the stretching, rolling and turning process again and again.

6. You don't need to knead a pastry or biscuit dough many times, but you may need to knead bread dough for 5–10 minutes. Once you have finished kneading bread dough, it should not feel sticky and should look a lot smoother than it did at the start.

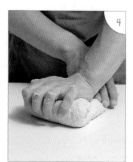
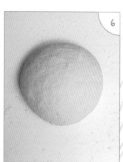

Proving bread

Bread contains an ingredient called yeast. When yeast is mixed with water and sugar, it releases a gas which is trapped by bread dough and makes it grow. This is what gives bread a light texture. Proving takes time, so you have to be patient.

1. Place your kneaded dough into a bowl and cover with cling film or a tea towel.

2. Leave in a warm place for 45 minutes or more. During this time, the dough will rise and become smoother as well.

3. Tip your proved and risen bread out onto a worktop. Try to keep it in one piece. Press it flat onto the worktop to knock out the air from it.

4. Shape your bread as directed in the recipe, then cover again with cling film or a tea towel to make sure it doesn't dry out, and leave in a warm place for 45 minutes–1 hour 30 minutes, or until the dough has about doubled in size and is jiggly.

Slicing a cake

I only have two round cake tins, so if I want to make a layer cake with four layers of sponge, I need to slice them in half. Check with your grown-up before doing this yourself. You need to be very careful when working with knives like this.

1. Lean down so you are at eye level with the cake.

2. Place one hand flat onto the top of the cake and use your other hand to hold a long serrated knife.

3. Cut a mark into the side of the cake halfway up the height of the cake. Turn the cake and make another mark on the same line. Do this around the cake, so there is a marked line all around it.

4. Cut slightly further into the cake, about 2cm (1"), following the guidelines of the mark. Turn the cake and repeat this all the way around.

5. Continue doing this, cutting slightly further into the cake each time until you eventually cut through the cake and split it into two layers.

6. Some key things to remember when doing this. Keep the cake at eye level to see you are holding the knife flat and cutting level. Always keep your other hand flat on top of the cake and away from the knife, so you don't cut yourself. Take your time.

Icing a cake

To ice a cake neatly, you need to cover it in two layers of icing. The first layer is very thin and is called a crumb coating or dirty ice. This layer locks in all the crumbs from the cake, so they don't show through when you cover it with the second, thicker layer of icing.

1. Add some icing to the top of your cake. Use a palette knife to spread this out into a very thin layer on the top of the cake, pushing the icing over the sides.

2. Spread the icing down the sides of the cake. Hold the palette knife flat against the side of the cake and drag it around the edge, keeping it pressed against the side of the cake to completely cover the sides in a thin layer of icing. You should still be able to see the cake through the icing after the dirty ice stage. Place it in the fridge to chill for at least 20 minutes.

3. Top your cake with the remaining icing. Spread it out over the top and sides as you did for the dirty ice.

4. This time you will have more icing to work with, so as you are spreading, you don't want the palette knife to be pressing into the side of the cake. Instead, spread out the icing by pushing it onto itself.

Filling a piping bag

Sometimes when piping, you can use piping nozzles which are special pieces of kit that allow you to pipe decorations with fancy patterns. If using a nozzle, you need to remember to fit the nozzle before you fill the bag. Cut a small opening in the bag and slide in the nozzle to do this. About half of the nozzle should be visible outside the bag. If you don't need a nozzle, you can fill the bag and then cut an opening into the bag after.

1. Open your piping bag and place it into a tall jug or container.
2. Fold the sides of the bag over the top edges of the container.
3. Fill the piping bag in the container with your mixture.
4. Lift the bag out of the container and shake it from the edges of the bag. This will push the filling down into the bag.
5. Twist the top of the bag above where the filling is and tie a knot in the excess bag or clip it shut with a clip to make sure it doesn't leak from that end.

Piping

There are lots of different piping designs you can try, but the technique of how you hold the bag and pipe stays the same.

1. Twist the top of the piping bag so it becomes tight, and the mixture starts moving towards the end of the bag.
2. Hold the twisted top end of the bag in your strong hand between your thumb and first finger. It should feel like your hand is wrapped around the mixture in the bag.

3. Lay your other hand at the side of the bag close to the opening.

4. To pipe, squeeze slightly firmer with your hand on the bag's top, and the mixture will begin to come out. Guide where you are piping with your other hand that is rested on the side of the bag. Don't squeeze with the guiding hand.

5. When you want to stop piping, stop squeezing with your top hand.

6. As you pipe, the bag will feel less tight. Stop and twist the top of the bag again until the bag feels tight, and repeat the piping.

7. Sometimes you can have quite a lot of mixture and the bag can be too big to handle. When this happens, make sure the back of the piping bag is tied or clipped shut. Squeeze some of the mixture towards the back of the bag so half is at the front and half is at the back. Twist the bag in the middle and place your strong hand behind the front portion of the mixture and pipe as instructed before. The mixture in the back of the bag can dangle over the back of your hand as you pipe with the front part of the mixture.

Zesting

The zest of citrus fruits is the colourful outer layer of skin. It adds a fantastic fresh taste to bakes.

1. Press a grater onto a flat board with your weak hand, holding it in place.

2. Hold a citrus fruit in your strong hand, and keeping your fingers away from the grater, gently drag one side of the fruit down against the grater.

3. Find a new part of the fruit and repeat this process until you have grated off all of the zest. Don't grate off any of the white pith underneath the zest, as this can be bitter.

Whipping cream

Whipping cream traps air in the mixture and makes it light and thick. You need to use double cream (heavy cream) or whipping cream. Single cream won't whip because it doesn't have enough fat content to trap the air. A risk of whipping cream is that you can overwhip it. However, a long-life cream alternative (such as Elmlea in the UK) will never overwhip, which is quite good to know.

1. Add the cream into a bowl. Whisk with an electric hand whisk on high speed until it turns into a thicker liquid.

2. Reduce the speed of the mixer to low because you don't want to overwhip the cream at this point. Whisk the cream until it thickens just enough to hold a trail in the cream.

3. Stop whisking at this point and gently stir the cream by hand with the beaters and the whisk turned off. Stir a couple of times until the cream is firm enough to just hold onto the beaters when lifted from the bowl.

4. If you keep whipping after this point, the cream will become grainy. If you overwhip the cream, you can keep beating it until it splits apart into solids and liquid. Sieve out the solids; this is butter.

Melting chocolate

You can melt chocolate over a pan of warm water (called a bain-marie) or in the microwave. The important thing to remember when melting chocolate is that you don't need to get it too hot for it to melt. It only needs to be warm.

TO MELT CHOCOLATE IN THE MICROWAVE

☆ Break it into chunks and place these in a microwave-safe bowl.

☆ Place in the microwave on full power for 30 seconds. Remove it from the microwave and stir.

☆ Repeat microwaving the chocolate for 30-second bursts and stirring until the chocolate is melted.

TO MELT CHOCOLATE IN A BAIN-MARIE

☆ Fill a small pan with a couple of centimetres of water and place over a low heat until it is just steaming.

☆ Break up the chocolate and place it in a heat-proof bowl that can sit on top of the pan without touching the water underneath.

☆ Place the bowl of chocolate over the warm water in the pan and stir until it is melted and smooth.

When waiting for chocolate to set, try to do this at room temperature and only put it in the fridge once it has nearly set at room temperature (20–30 minutes). Chocolate will set better if given time to set at room temperature.

CHAPTER 1
SAVOURY BAKES

SAUSAGE ROLL WREATH

GFO

Growing up in Edinburgh, we always got half days from school on Fridays, finishing at lunchtime. As a treat, loads of families would line up at the local bakery or butchers to get a sausage roll for lunch at the end of the week. It was a treat that would always excite me!

Crispy, buttery pastry wrapped around well-seasoned sausage meat means a sausage roll will be a crowd-pleaser at any lunch or picnic. This recipe takes the standard sausage roll and makes it even more special by turning it into a showstopping wreath. The shaping adds a layer of difficulty, but don't be worried, it's quite a forgiving bake to handle and shape. You can reshape the sausage roll a few times if at first it isn't looking quite as you want.

One important thing to note before you get baking: make sure you give your hands and equipment a really good wash after handling raw meat to keep safe and hygienic in the kitchen.

TIME REQUIRED

20 minutes prep
15 minutes chilling
40 minutes baking

BAKING CHALLENGE

INGREDIENTS

400–500g (1lb-1lb 2oz) sausage meat (or 6–8 sausages)

375g (13oz) shop-bought puff pastry

1 egg, beaten

METHOD

1. Preheat the oven to 190°C fan (410°F/gas 6).
2. If using sausage meat, add this into a bowl. If using sausages, use scissors to cut down the skin on the outside of the sausage and peel off from the sausage meat. Add the meat into a bowl and discard the skins. Give the sausage meat a quick mix in the bowl with a spoon.
3. Roll out the puff pastry on a sheet of baking paper into a rectangle about 30cm x 40cm (12" x 16"). If using pre-rolled pastry, you probably won't need to roll it out further.
4. Lay the sausage meat in a log along the long side of the pastry, about a third of the way down from the top. Try to make it quite even in thickness across the pastry.

5. Brush the pastry on the side below the sausage meat with egg wash.

6. Roll the top portion of pastry tightly around the sausage meat to meet the egg-washed pastry underneath. Continue rolling the log until you reach the end of the pastry. Place on a baking tray lined with baking paper and chill in the fridge for at least 15 minutes.

7. Take the sausage roll out of the fridge. Trim off the edges and cut slits into the log at about 2.5cm (1") intervals, not cutting all the way to the back of the roll, so it stays in one piece.

8. Curl the log around to create a ring. Brush a little egg wash onto one of the edges and try to stick them together.

9. Gently twist each sausage roll section so the sausage meat faces up.

10. Brush any visible parts of the pastry with egg wash. Slide onto a baking tray and bake in the oven for 40–45 minutes until very deep golden.

Bake it your own

✗ After egg washing the pastry, you can sprinkle over some seeds to make a crunchy, nutty finish to the bake. It's also nice to sprinkle over some flaky salt.

✗ You can turn this into a Scottish sausage roll by replacing 200–300g (7-10oz) of sausage meat with haggis.

Make this gluten-free

✗ Replace the puff pastry with shop-bought gluten-free puff pastry.

✗ Make sure the sausage meat you use is gluten-free.

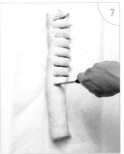

SWEET POTATO BAKES

If you or your friends are veggie and can't enjoy the sausage roll recipe on the previous page, you must try this instead (you've got to try it even if you aren't veggie). The sweet potato filling is flavoured with coconut milk and a jerk spice blend. 'Jerk' is a cooking style common in Jamaica, where the jerk marinade or spice blend is most commonly added to chicken and pork before cooking over coals or a fire pit.

This recipe is definitely not authentic to Jamaican or jerk cooking. However, the warming spices of jerk with the sweet potato and creamy coconut milk make for a delicious filling and a very warming and satisfying lunch or dinner.

If you don't need to make 8 portions, you can halve all the ingredients, only use one pack of puff pastry and easily make 4 bakes. The bakes can also be frozen fully prepared before baking. You just need to give them 10–15 minutes more in the oven and make sure they are piping hot in the centre before serving.

MAKES 8

TIME REQUIRED
30 minutes prep
20 minutes chilling
30 minutes baking

BAKING CHALLENGE

INGREDIENTS

500g (1lb 2oz) sweet potato, peeled

2 teaspoons dried thyme

1 tablespoon jerk spice blend

2 tablespoons light brown sugar

½ teaspoon salt

200ml (¾ cup + 2 tablespoons) coconut milk

1 tin kidney beans, drained (240g/8½oz)

200g (7oz) frozen peas

2 packs ready-rolled puff pastry (about 750g/1lb 10oz)

1 egg, beaten

METHOD

1. Preheat the oven to 190°C fan (410°F/gas 6).

MAKE THE FILLING

1. Dice the sweet potato into about 1cm (½") cubes. Add this to a pan with the thyme, jerk seasoning, sugar, salt and coconut milk.

2. Bring this to a bubble, cover and leave over a low heat to simmer for about 10 minutes. After this, the potato should be quite soft.

3. Remove the lid from the pan and continue to cook, occasionally stirring, until you can't see any coconut milk remaining.

4. Roughly mash the sweet potato, then stir through the kidney beans and still-frozen peas. Spread this out onto a shallow tray and chill in the fridge for about 10 minutes until room temperature.

ASSEMBLE THE PIES

1. Unroll the sheets of puff pastry. From each sheet, cut out 8 rectangles by splitting the sheets in two then cutting each half into 4. You should have 16 rectangles of pastry.

2. Spoon a mound of filling onto 8 rectangles of pastry, leaving a 1cm (½") border of pastry around the filling.

3. Brush some egg wash on the pastry border of the filled rectangles.

4. Top each filled rectangle with another rectangle of pastry. Firmly press the two pieces of pastry together so they stick. Press the edges of pastry together with the back of a fork. You can trim off the rough edges of the pastry at this stage if you like.

Make this gluten-free

Replace the puff pastry with shop-bought gluten-free puff pastry.

5. Brush some egg wash over the pastry. Use the back of a fork to gently drag over the pastry to create a pattern when baked. Sprinkle over some extra dried thyme and flaky salt.

6. Bake for about 30 minutes, until deeply golden brown. Serve hot, straight from the oven, or reheat in the oven for about 10 minutes if eating later.

TOAD IN THE HOLE

You will be glad to hear there are no toads in this recipe despite what the name says. It's a very odd name for a dish, but I suppose the 'toad' refers to the sausages, and the hole is the Yorkshire pudding in which the toads sit. My mum has always made this for us since we were very young, and we continue to love it. During lockdown, my brother would make Toad in the Hole every week for our family. It's such a comforting and delicious dinner for me, and it always got me excited to know this was coming for dinner.

Toad in the Hole was also one of the first dinners my brother and I would make for our parents when we were young. It doesn't take long to prepare and doesn't require a lot of washing up, so it's a great first step to taking on some dinnertime cooking responsibilities at home.

SERVES 4–6

TIME REQUIRED
10 minutes prep
45 minutes baking

BAKING CHALLENGE

INGREDIENTS

1 tablespoon oil

8–12 sausages (you can use vegetarian sausages)

125g (4½oz) cornflour

½ teaspoon baking powder

½ teaspoon salt

3 eggs

200ml (¾ cup + 2 tablespoons) milk

METHOD

1. Grease a roasting tin measuring roughly 23cm x 33cm (9" x 13") with a tablespoon of oil, rubbing it around with a piece of kitchen roll. Preheat the oven to 200°C fan (425°F/gas 7).

2. Add the sausages into the roasting tin. Prick the sausages a couple of times with a fork to prevent them splitting in the oven. Bake the sausages in the oven for about 10 minutes.

3. Whilst the sausages are in the oven, make the batter. Add the cornflour, baking powder and salt into a mixing bowl. Crack in the eggs and about a quarter of the milk and whisk until a smooth, fairly thick batter. Add the rest of the milk slowly whilst whisking until you have a smooth, thin batter.

4. Remove the sausages from the oven and flip them to ensure they aren't stuck to the tin and are evenly spaced out.

5. Whisk the batter you have just made and pour into the tin around the sausages, covering the base of the tin.

6. Bake in the oven for about 30–35 minutes until dark golden and well risen.

Make this gluten-free

Make sure the sausage meat you use is gluten-free.

Bake it your own

☆ Make individual Toad in the Holes. Add a teaspoon of oil into the holes of a 12-hole muffin tray, and add half a sausage into each hole. Bake for 10 minutes before removing and pouring the batter into the muffin holes till half full. Bake for a further 20 minutes until well-risen and golden.

☆ Make standard Yorkshire puddings. Add 1 teaspoon of oil into the holes of a 12-hole muffin tray. Place this in the oven to preheat for about 5–10 minutes. Pour the batter into the preheated tray from a jug to fill the holes about half full. Bake for about 20 minutes until well-risen and golden.

HARISSA ROAST VEGETABLE GALETTE

GFO

If you want to try something a little spicy, this is a great dinner. A galette is a flat tart that is easier to shape than something in a tin. It's meant to look a little rustic, so if your pastry cracks and looks a bit wonky, that's okay.

Harissa gives a bold flavour to this bake. It's a North African pepper paste that you can pick up in the supermarket, made with chillies, garlic and many spices, so it packs a big flavour punch. If this flavour is new to you, I am very excited for you to try it! It can be a little spicy, but this is why you make the yoghurt drizzle. The yoghurt will help cool your mouth down if it gets too hot. You can eat this hot for a family dinner or take it with you for a cold lunch or picnic. It's equally delicious either way.

SERVES 4–6

TIME REQUIRED
45 minutes prep
1 hour baking

BAKING CHALLENGE

INGREDIENTS

For the wholemeal pastry

100g (3½oz) butter, chilled and diced

200g (7oz) wholemeal flour

½ teaspoon salt

1 egg yolk

1 tablespoon + 1 teaspoon water

For the filling

1 large carrot, peeled and chopped into 8 pieces

1 large red pepper, washed, deseeded and sliced into 16 pieces

1 large courgette, washed and cut into 1cm (½") thick slices

2 red onions, peeled and sliced into 6 wedges

3–4 tablespoons harissa paste (depending on how spicy you like it!)

1 tablespoon olive oil

½ teaspoon salt

150g (5oz) hummus

1 egg yolk (for glazing)

For the yoghurt drizzle (optional)

½ bunch coriander

100g (3½oz) yoghurt

½ lemon, juice

Pinch of salt

METHOD

1. Preheat the oven to 180°C fan (400°F/gas 6).

MAKE THE PASTRY

1. Rub the butter into the flour and salt with your fingertips until the texture resembles fine breadcrumbs.
2. Add the egg yolk and water and use a blunt table knife to stir the mixture together until it begins to form large clumps.
3. Use your hands to press the mixture into a smooth ball of dough.
4. Press the dough into a flat disc on a piece of cling film, wrap tightly and chill in the fridge for at least 20 minutes whilst you prepare the veg.

PREPARE THE FILLING

1. Chop the veg into chunky pieces as directed in the ingredients list (it doesn't matter if you are precise with chopping!).
2. Add the veg into a large roasting tin and mix through the harissa, oil and salt until all the veg is evenly covered. Roast in the oven for about 25 minutes until the veg softens a little and picks up some colour.

ASSEMBLE THE TART

1. Roll out the chilled pastry on a sheet of baking paper into a circle about 30cm (12") in diameter. If the pastry has been in the fridge for more than 20 minutes, leave it out at room temperature for 5–10 minutes before rolling to make it easier to work with.
2. Spread the hummus over the pastry, leaving a 3cm (1") border around the pastry.
3. Pile the roasted veg onto the hummus. It should be cool enough to handle at this point.
4. Lift the uncovered edge of the pastry at one point and press it over the edge of the veg. Repeat this around the tart, leaving the centre of the veg open but covering the filling at the edge.
5. Brush the edge of the pastry with the egg yolk. Bake for 30–35 minutes until the pastry is golden. Leave to cool on the tray for about 5 minutes before sliding onto your serving board.

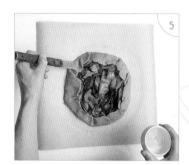

MAKE THE YOGHURT DRIZZLE

1. Chop the coriander as finely as you can.

2. Stir the coriander into the yoghurt with a small pinch of salt and some lemon juice. Taste the yoghurt and add more lemon juice until you like the flavour. Serve this alongside slices of the galette.

Bake it your own

For a quicker dinner, use ready-made puff pastry instead of making your own wholemeal pastry.

Make this gluten-free

Replace the wholemeal flour in the pastry with gluten-free plain flour and ½ teaspoon xanthan gum.

FLUFFY PANCAKES

You need a go-to pancake recipe when you want a breakfast treat on the weekend, or to have 'breakfast for dinner' as a way to switch up your evening meal. There are a few types of pancakes. The main ones in the UK are Scotch pancakes, crêpes and American pancakes, although there are loads more pancake-style bakes across the world. French crêpes are very thin and flat. Scotch pancakes are thicker and smaller than crêpes. American pancakes are like Scotch pancakes but lighter and fluffier – and this one is my absolute favourite.

The baking powder (also contained in the self-raising flour) in these pancakes starts to bubble and release carbon dioxide when it gets wet in the batter. It bubbles even more when you heat the batter by cooking it in the pan. This means the pancakes puff up in the pan, and that is what makes them deliciously light and fluffy.

Pancakes can be savoury or sweet, or a bit of both. See the 'Bake it your own' section to see some ideas of what you could serve with the pancakes. Pancakes are a lot more versatile than people often think, so you can go wild with the toppings and pair them with loads of dishes. If you think it will be tasty, go for it!

MAKES ABOUT 12 MEDIUM-SIZED PANCAKES

TIME REQUIRED

5 minutes prep
20 minutes cooking

BAKING CHALLENGE

INGREDIENTS

250g (9oz) self-raising flour

1½ teaspoons baking powder

½ teaspoon salt

30g (1oz) caster sugar (optional depending on sweet or savoury)

2 eggs

250ml (1 cup + 1 tablespoon) milk

50g (1¾oz) butter

Oil and butter for cooking

METHOD

1. Add the flour, baking powder, salt and sugar into a mixing bowl. Add the eggs and milk, and whisk until combined into a batter. It doesn't have to be very smooth.

2. Melt the butter in the microwave and drizzle into the batter whilst whisking to combine. Stop whisking once combined.

3. Place a large frying pan over medium heat with one teaspoon of oil and a small knob of butter. When the butter looks frothy, add the batter into the pan:

use about 4 tablespoons (¼ cup) of batter for each pancake. You can cook multiple at a time, but make sure they have a little space between them in the pan.

4. Cook on one side for about 3 minutes, until lots of bubbles have appeared on the surface and popped. Then flip and cook on the other side for a further minute.

5. Repeat the cooking process with the rest of the batter, and add a little more butter and oil before cooking each new batch. If the pan starts to smoke, carefully wipe out the old butter and oil with kitchen roll before cooking the next batch (you can ask a grown-up to do this for you). Stack the cooked pancakes on a plate and cover in a tea towel to keep warm while cooking the remaining pancakes.

Bake it your own

✶ Some pancake topping suggestions:

　✶ Top the pancake batter with blueberries whilst frying in the pan before flipping. Serve alongside whipped cream and a drizzle of honey.

　✶ Cook bacon in the oven and serve with maple syrup.

　✶ Top savoury pancakes with the afternoon tea sandwich fillings from page 167.

Make this gluten-free

✶ Replace the self-raising flour with gluten-free self-raising flour.

✶ Ensure the baking powder is gluten-free.

BEEF STEW & DUMPLINGS

GFO

I was wondering if this recipe felt a little out of place in this book, but I couldn't bring myself to remove it because I love stew and dumplings too much. Making a stew is real proper cooking, and learning the techniques of chopping, searing and braising through this stew can be used in so many other dishes that you will cook in the future.

The stew is really rich and meaty. You cook the dumplings in the top of the stew, and they puff up but stay a little stodgy and very satisfying. This is the most comforting hug in a bowl you could look for on a cold, dark winter night.

SERVES 4–6

TIME REQUIRED
30 minutes prep
2 hours cooking

BAKING CHALLENGE

INGREDIENTS

For the stew

2 tablespoons olive oil

500g (1lb 2oz) diced stewing beef

½ teaspoon salt

2 onions, peeled and chopped into bitesized chunks

2 large carrots, peeled and chopped into bitesized chunks

1 leek, washed and sliced

2 garlic cloves, minced

1 tin (400g/14oz) butterbeans, including liquid

1 tablespoon dried thyme

1 beef stock cube

1 tablespoon balsamic vinegar

200ml (¾ cup + 2 tablespoons) gravy, from granules

400ml (1½ cups + 3 tablespoons) water

2 tablespoons cornflour, mixed with 4 tablespoons water

For the dumplings

150g (5oz) self-raising flour

½ teaspoon salt

75g (2½oz) vegetable or beef suet

90ml (⅓ cup + 1 tablespoon) water

Make this gluten-free

☆ Ensure the gravy granules you use are gluten-free.

☆ Ensure the stock cube is gluten-free.

☆ Replace the self-raising flour in the dumplings with gluten-free self-raising flour.

☆ Ensure the suet product you use for the dumplings is gluten-free.

METHOD

MAKE THE STEW

1. Preheat the oven to 140°C fan (325°F/ gas 3).

2. Place a casserole dish on the hob over medium-high heat. Add the oil, then add the beef to the hot dish in a single layer, and sprinkle over the salt. Let the beef fry without touching it for about 2 minutes, so it browns on the bottom. Stir the beef and leave it to cook on the next side for 2 minutes.

3. Add the chopped onions, carrots, leek and minced garlic to the beef and cook for about three minutes, stirring occasionally.

4. Add the butterbeans with their liquid, thyme, stock cube, vinegar, gravy and water. With a wooden spoon, scrape the bottom of the pan to pick up any brown bits that have formed on the base of the casserole (this contains lots of flavour).

5. Bring this to a simmer before adding the cornflour mixed with water. Stir this through. It should thicken slightly.

6. Put the lid onto the casserole before placing it in the oven for about 1–1½ hours while you make the dumplings.

MAKE THE DUMPLINGS

1. Add the flour, salt and suet to a bowl. Add the water and mix through with a table knife until it forms into a soft dough.

2. Take tablespoon-sized portions of dough and roll them into a rough ball in your hands. Place on a floured tray until you have shaped all the dough.

3. Remove the casserole from the oven and gently place the dough balls on the stew, evenly spread apart. (If the dough is too soft to roll balls, use two spoons to scrape spoonfuls of the dough onto the stew).

4. Cover the stew and place it back in the oven for about 20 minutes.

5. Serve with some greens on the side.

Bake it your own

A stew is a perfect dish to use up any odd bits and pieces of vegetables that are filling up your fridge and possibly going a little past their best. Feel free to add any chopped-up spare veg to the stew in addition to the carrots, onions and leeks, or to replace them.

CHAPTER 2
BREAD

my first loaf

SIMPLE CRUSTY LOAF

Few things in life are better than bread and butter!

This is a very simple bread recipe and shows how basic the ingredients in bread are. It is important to use strong bread flour, as this contains more gluten, a protein that helps the bread rise and makes it springy, not crumbly. The yeast is the special ingredient in bread that magically makes the dough rise. It releases the gas carbon dioxide, which gets trapped in the dough and pushes it to grow. Yeast is what makes bread light and airy instead of dense and stodgy. The oil in this bread is not necessary. I use it for a bit of flavour and to make the crumb slightly softer; however, you can replace it with an extra tablespoon of water.

I have given two ways to shape this basic bread dough. One is to make a loaf in a tin, which is perfect for sandwiches. The other is a free-form loaf that looks like it's straight from an artisanal bakery.

MAKES 1 LOAF

TIME REQUIRED
20 minutes prep
1 hour 30 minutes proving
40 minutes baking

BAKING CHALLENGE

INGREDIENTS

400g (14oz) strong white bread flour

1 teaspoon salt

2 teaspoons active dried yeast

1 tablespoon olive oil

240ml (1 cup) water

METHOD

1. Add the flour, salt and yeast into a mixing bowl. Add the oil and water and stir with a table knife until combined into a shaggy dough with some dry patches of flour.

2. Tip this out onto a work surface and knead to work in the dry patches of flour. Then continue to knead for about 10 minutes until a lot smoother and springy. Place back in the bowl, cover with a tea towel and leave aside for at least 30 minutes, ideally about 1 hour. It will rise in this time and develop flavour.

3. Tip the dough out of the bowl onto a work surface and press it flat with your palms.

TO SHAPE A ROUND LOAF

1. Stretch the edge of the dough at a point and pull it into the centre of the dough. Repeat this all around the dough and pinch all the folds together on top of the loaf.

2. Flip the loaf over onto the joins of the edges to show a smooth top. Press the sides of your hands into the base of the dough whilst turning it slightly to encourage the loaf to be round.

3. Gently lift the dough onto a baking tray lined with baking paper and sprinkle the top of the loaf with flour. Loosely cover with cling film or a clean tea towel.

4. Set aside in a warm place for 45 minutes–1 hour 30 minutes until nearly doubled in size and puffy.

5. When proved and ready to bake, sprinkle with some extra flour from a height, then use a sharp knife to cut four slashes on the top of the dough to create a big square.

TO SHAPE A SANDWICH LOAF

1. Lightly grease a 900g (2lb) loaf tin with a little butter or oil. Line the base and long sides of the tin with a single long piece of baking paper overhanging the sides.

2. Fold over the edges of the flattened dough, so it is as wide as the tin is long.

3. Roll up the dough from one side into a big sausage shape. Lift the dough and place it into the tin seam-side down.

4. Sprinkle flour over the top of the dough from a height and cover the tin with cling film or a clean tea towel.

5. Set aside in a warm place for 45 minutes–1 hour 30 minutes until nearly doubled in size and puffy. It should be peeking over the sides of the tin.

6. When proved and ready to bake, use a sharp knife to carefully cut three slashes into the top of the bread.

BAKE THE LOAVES

1. When the loaf has been proving for about 40 minutes, preheat the oven to 210°C fan (450°F/gas 7) for a super crusty loaf or 190°C fan (410°F/gas 6) for a softer loaf and place a roasting tin in the bottom of the oven.

2. When the dough is ready to bake, fill the roasting tin in the bottom of the oven with about 500ml (2 cups) of hot water. Place the dough in the oven at the same time and let it bake in the steamy oven for 25 minutes. Then remove the roasting tin with water and continue to bake for a further 15–20 minutes until it is a deep golden brown. You can tell if it's baked by holding the loaf on its side with oven gloves and knocking on the base with your knuckles. It should sound hollow.

3. Leave your bread to cool completely on a wire rack before slicing to allow the crumb to set. Patience is key with bread!

GLUTEN-FREE LOAF

My brother is gluten-intolerant, so I have always been interested in baking gluten-free treats for him to enjoy. But I always struggled trying to make gluten-free bread. Gluten is essential in bread making, so a gluten-free bread recipe is very different. I made my first good gluten-free loaf with a recipe from a fantastic gluten-free cook called Becky Excell, which, along with other recipes I have explored, heavily informed my starting point for developing this recipe. If you are interested in gluten-free baking, I highly recommend her books.

There are a couple of specialist ingredients that you need for this bread:

☆ **Xanthan gum** is a thickener that helps prevent the bread from becoming too crumbly. You can buy this in the free-from section of most supermarkets.

☆ **Psyllium husk powder** helps make the dough stretchy, like gluten does in a standard loaf. You can buy psyllium husk powder online.

This bread comes out with a light, springy texture, which is often lacking in gluten-free bread. If you or one of your friends is gluten-intolerant, I am sure this bread will be a great treat.

MAKES 1 LOAF

TIME REQUIRED
15 minutes prep
45 minutes proving
45 minutes baking

BAKING CHALLENGE

INGREDIENTS

Butter or oil for greasing

350g (12½oz) gluten-free plain flour

1½ teaspoons xanthan gum

20g (¾oz) psyllium husk powder

1 teaspoon salt

2 teaspoons fast-action dried yeast

400ml (1½ cups + 3 tablespoons) warm water

20g (¾oz) honey

1 egg

2 teaspoons lemon juice

METHOD

1. Lightly grease a 900g (2lb) loaf tin with a little butter or oil. Line the base and long sides of the tin with a single long piece of baking paper overhanging the sides.

2. Add the flour, xanthan gum, psyllium husk powder, salt and yeast to a mixing bowl and mix.

3. Add the warm water, honey, egg and lemon juice to the bowl. Stir to combine, then beat with an electric mixer for 4–5 minutes. It should look like a very thick, gloopy batter. When you are beating, only beat the top of the batter, then use a spatula to

scrape up the bottom of the mixture before beating again. If you use the whisk at the bottom of the bowl, the mixture will climb up the whisk and cover the mixer.

4. Pour this thick, sticky mass into the lined tin and cover with a lightly oiled piece of cling film. Leave this in a warm place to prove for about 45 minutes–1 hour 30 minutes. It is ready to bake when it has grown by about 50 per cent, or the domed top of the loaf is sitting above the edge of the tin.

5. About 40 minutes into proving, preheat the oven to 210°C fan (450°F/ gas 7). Place a roasting tin in the bottom of the oven at the same time.

6. Once the loaf has proved, dust it generously with more gluten-free flour and cut a few slashes into the top with a sharp knife.

7. Place the bread in the oven. At the same time, fill the roasting tray with about 500ml (2 cups) of water. This will create steam. Bake the bread in the steamy oven for about 25 minutes before removing the tray of water and continuing to bake for a further 20–25 minutes or until the bread is very dark on top.

8. Use the baking paper to lift the loaf out of the tin, lay it on its side and tap the base. The loaf should make a hollow knocking sound as you tap. If it doesn't, put it back in the oven to bake for 5–10 more minutes.

9. Once baked, leave it to cool completely on a wire rack before slicing into it.

Bake it your own

Fold 100g (3½oz) of seeds into the mixture with a spatula after beating it with the electric whisk.

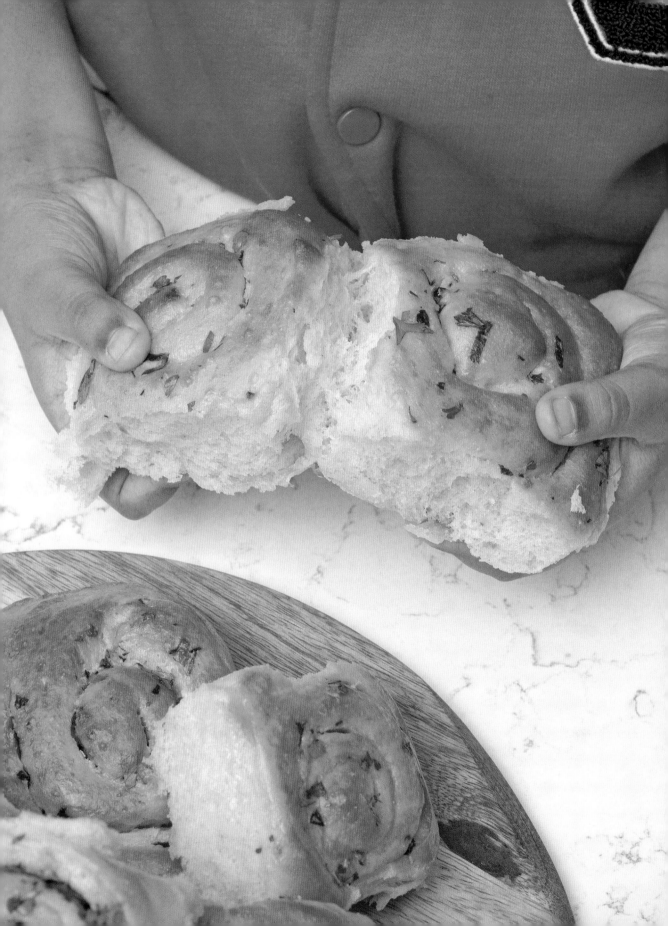

TEAR & SHARE GARLIC SWIRLS

Who doesn't love garlic bread?!

This garlic bread is next level! The dough is super soft, and when you eat the buns fresh from the oven, it is something very special. If you leave the buns for a couple of days, you can gently warm them covered with aluminium foil in the oven with a light sprinkling of water for 5–10 minutes or in the microwave for 30 seconds.

This bread is made with a tangzhong, a mixture of flour and water cooked into a paste often used in breads from Japan and elsewhere in Asia. This adds more moisture to the dough and makes the bread extra soft.

MAKES 12 BUNS

TIME REQUIRED
30 minutes prep
1 hour 45 minutes proving
20 minutes baking

BAKING CHALLENGE

INGREDIENTS

For the tangzhong
150ml (½ cup + 2 tablespoons) water

30g (1oz) strong bread flour

For the dough
600g (1lb 5oz) strong bread flour

2 teaspoons fast-action dried yeast

1 teaspoon salt

200ml (¾ cup + 2 tablespoons) milk

1 egg

50g (1¾oz) butter, very soft

For the filling
100g (3½oz) butter, very soft

8–12 garlic cloves, crushed in a garlic press

10g (½oz) parsley, finely chopped

½ teaspoon salt

1 egg, beaten

METHOD

TO MAKE THE TANGZHONG

1. Mix the flour and water in a small pan until smooth.
2. Place over high heat, stirring until the mixture begins to bubble and becomes thick.
3. Transfer to a bowl, cover the surface with cling film and let cool to room temperature or just warm.

TO MAKE THE DOUGH

1. Add all the ingredients for the dough into a mixing bowl with the tangzhong.
2. Mix with a spoon until a dough begins to form, then squeeze the dough together in your hands.
3. Once it has become a single ball of dough with a couple of dry patches of flour, tip it onto a worktop.
4. Knead the dough for about 10 minutes. It will stop sticking to the table and will become far smoother through kneading, although it doesn't have to be completely smooth at the end.
5. Place back into the mixing bowl, cover with a tea towel or cling film and leave to prove for 30 minutes–1 hour whilst you make the filling. It will rise and become smoother in this time.

TO MAKE THE FILLING AND ASSEMBLE

1. Mix the garlic, parsley and salt through the butter and set aside.

2. Turn the dough out onto a lightly floured surface. Roll out into a large rectangle about 40cm x 25cm (16" x 10").

3. As you roll, the dough will want to shrink back slightly. As it does this, gently lift the dough, lay it back down and let it shrink back to where it wants to go for about 20 seconds before rolling again and repeating the process.

4. Spread the soft butter mixture all over the dough.

5. Roll the dough into a tight spiral from one of the long edges.

6. Cut the roll into 12 slices.

7. Place the rolls into a large baking tin (approx. 23cm x 33cm/9" x 13" or bigger), lined on the base with baking paper, in three rows of four. The rolls shouldn't quite touch each other.

8. Cover the tin and leave to prove in a warm place for 45 minutes–1 hour 15 minutes or until the buns have doubled in size, are very puffy and begin to touch one another.

9. Whilst the dough is proving, preheat the oven to 170°C fan (375°F/gas 5). Next to the preheating oven is a perfect warm place to leave the buns to prove.

10. Brush the proved buns with beaten egg and bake for 20–25 minutes until they are golden on top.

11. Brush the buns with a wee bit of extra melted butter and leave to cool for at least 10 minutes before digging in warm or leaving to cool completely.

Bake it your own

Shape and bake this dough (without the filling) as shown in the Simple Crusty Loaf recipe (page 49) to make a delicious soft sandwich loaf.

BAGELS

I love the chewy texture of bagels. This comes from a rather strange technique that you wouldn't expect when making bread: boiling the dough before baking it. Boiling the bagels in water with bicarbonate of soda makes them bake with a chewy texture and go a very attractive deep bronze colour in the oven.

Homemade bagels beat the taste and texture of shop-bought bagels every time. However, you will never be able to get the consistent shaping of bagels that you see in the shop when making them at home. I'm happy to eat some slightly wonky bagels when they taste this good.

MAKES 8

TIME REQUIRED
30 minutes prep
1 hour resting
20 minutes baking

BAKING CHALLENGE

INGREDIENTS

400g (14oz) strong white bread flour

2 teaspoons fast-action dried yeast

1 teaspoons salt

20g (¾oz) honey

230ml (1 cup + 1 teaspoon) water

2 tablespoons bicarbonate of soda (for boiling, not the dough)

100g (3½oz) seeds, for topping

METHOD

1. Add the flour, yeast and salt to a mixing bowl. Add the honey and water and stir until nearly fully combined with a table knife.

2. Tip out onto a work surface and knead for about 10 minutes until the dough is smooth. This is quite a workout as the dough is stiff. It might be good to take turns for a minute each with a partner!

3. Place the dough back into the bowl, cover and leave aside for 30 minutes or longer.

4. Turn out the dough onto a work surface, flatten with your hands and cut into 8 portions. You can weigh the portions. They should be about 80g (2¾oz) each.

5. Flatten each portion of dough and pull the edges of the dough into the centre and pinch together.

6. Flip the dough onto the pinched side and cover with a cupped hand. Gently press onto the dough and rotate to create a ball. Cover with clingfilm or a clean tea towel and set aside for 10 minutes.

7. At this point, preheat the oven to 200°C fan (425°F/ gas 7). Line two baking trays with baking paper.

8. To make the bagel hole, press your finger through the centre of a ball of dough. Gently open the hole and stretch it out by spinning the bagel on your finger. The hole should be about 3–4cm (1–1½") wide. Cover the shaped bagel for a further 15 minutes whilst repeating the shaping process for the rest of the bagels.

9. Bring a large pot of water to the boil and add the bicarbonate of soda.

10. Gently lay two bagels into the water and boil for 1 minute before flipping the bagel over. Boil for a further minute on the other side.

11. Remove the bagels from the water with a slotted spoon and lay them on a wire rack for 2 minutes. Cover a plate with the seeds. Take one of the cooling bagels and press one side into the seeds whilst it's still slightly damp from the boiling. Place back on the cooling rack as you repeat the boiling and dipping process with the rest of the bagels.

12. Once all the bagels have been boiled and topped, place them onto the baking trays lined with baking paper and bake for about 20 minutes and a very dark golden colour.

Bake it your own

- Top the bagels with any seeds you like. Poppy seeds and sesame seeds are classics.

- Make cinnamon raisin bagels by adding 1 teaspoon of cinnamon to the dough and kneading in 75g (2½oz) of raisins at the end of the kneading steps.

DARK SODA BREAD

Sometimes you want a loaf of bread but don't have the time to wait for it to prove. This is where soda bread comes in. Soda bread doesn't contain yeast. Instead, the bread rises in the oven because of the bicarbonate of soda which produces carbon dioxide when combined with acid and heat. It's kind of like a giant scone.

This bread also doesn't need a knead. Try to not mix the dough too much as this will make it heavy and thick instead of light and soft.

MAKES 1 LOAF

TIME REQUIRED
10 minutes prep
45 minutes baking

BAKING CHALLENGE

INGREDIENTS

300g (10½oz) plain flour

100g (3½oz) rye flour

1 teaspoon salt

1 teaspoon bicarbonate of soda

50g (1¾oz) butter

30g (1oz) honey

30g (1oz) black treacle

250ml (1 cup) buttermilk (or 210ml/1 cup + 2 tablespoons milk and 1 tablespoon lemon juice)

30g (1oz) oats, for sprinkling

METHOD

1. Preheat the oven to 180°C fan (400°F/gas 6). Line a baking tray with baking paper.
2. Add the plain flour, rye flour, salt and bicarb into a mixing bowl. Add the butter and rub in with your fingertips to a breadcrumb texture.
3. Add the honey, treacle and buttermilk, and stir together with a table knife into a dough. Knead a couple of times in the bowl to combine any dry patches into the dough. Don't knead too much.
4. Sprinkle the oats over your worktop. Lift the dough out of the bowl and form it into a big rough ball in your hands. Place the dough onto the oats and roll it around in the oats to coat the outside.
5. Lift the dough onto the baking tray. Press the dough into a round loaf shape on the paper if it's a little wonky.
6. Press a large knife or bench scraper into the dough through the middle, pressing three quarters of the way down through the dough. Do this once more to create a cross.
7. Bake for about 45 minutes until deep brown on top.
8. Leave to cool completely on a wire rack before enjoying.

FAST FLATBREADS

GFO

Soda bread is quick to make, but these are even faster! Only three ingredients needed (with the option to add herbs and spices). About 3 minutes of mixing and then 3 minutes of cooking, and you can have your first flatbread hot and ready to eat. When they are warm, they are super pillowy and soft and satisfying to eat with curry, stew or dips.

MAKES 4

TIME REQUIRED
10 minutes prep
15 minutes cooking

BAKING CHALLENGE

INGREDIENTS

250g (9oz) self-raising flour

½ teaspoon salt

1 teaspoon dried mixed herbs
(optional)

225g (8oz) natural yoghurt

Make this gluten-free

Substitute the self-raising flour for gluten-free self-raising flour.

METHOD

1. Add the flour, salt and herbs (if using) to a mixing bowl and stir together. Add the yoghurt and use a wooden spoon or spatula to mix and press the mixture into a rough dough.

2. Get your hand into the bowl and give it a couple of kneads to ensure all the flour is well combined.

3. Depending on how thick or loose your yoghurt is, you may need to add more flour if the dough is too sticky to handle or more yoghurt if the dough is very dry and cracking. You want the dough to be quite soft and slightly sticky but not unworkable.

4. Tip the dough out onto a well-floured surface and cut it into four portions.

5. Roll out each portion quite thin to about ½cm (¼") on a well-floured surface. Move the dough frequently as you roll and add more flour underneath if it begins to stick to the worktop, or dust the top of the dough with some flour if it sticks to the rolling pin.

6. Place a large flat frying pan over medium heat. Add one of your flatbreads to the pan and cook on one side for about 2 minutes. The dough should have nice brown patches all over after 2 minutes. Flip and cook on the other side for 1 minute until it picks up a nice deep brown colour on some patches (the colouring is never as even on the second side).

7. Repeat the cooking process with the rest of the flatbreads. Whilst you are cooking the other portions, keep the cooked flatbreads warm on a plate covered in a clean tea towel stacked on each other. Alternatively, you can reheat the flatbreads for about 20–30 seconds in the microwave.

CHAPTER 3

SWEET DOUGH

RAINBOW BUNS

This recipe is inspired by two different sweet breads that I think are amazing. Both the breads have a soft, slightly sweet dough sitting underneath a sweet, crunchy topping. The first of the inspiring breads is called concha and is a classic bread from Mexico. The crunchy, often colourful, topping on these buns is marked into the shape of a shell and gives the name to this bread because 'concha' means 'shell' in Spanish. I have taken the topping of a concha and put it on these rainbow buns.

The second bread that has inspired these buns is the pineapple bun from Hong Kong. The bread component of my recipe is inspired by the style of bread that makes a pineapple bun. It contains a tangzhong, a mixture of flour cooked in water which makes this bread amazingly soft.

Bread is often quite brown and possibly a little boring in appearance. Adding the rainbow colours to this bread through the crunchy sweet toppings makes these buns just that bit different to most bread you might bake.

MAKES 6 BUNS

TIME REQUIRED
30 minutes prep
1 hour 30 minutes proving
20 minutes baking

BAKING CHALLENGE

INGREDIENTS

For the tangzhong
15g (½oz) strong bread flour
75ml (¼ cup + 1 tablespoon) water

For the dough
300g (10½oz) strong bread flour
1½ teaspoons fast-action dried yeast
½ teaspoon salt
20g (¾oz) caster sugar
125ml (½ cup) milk
30g (1oz) butter, very soft

For the topping
60g (2oz) butter, softened
60g (2oz) caster sugar
60g (2oz) plain flour
Gel food colours

METHOD

TO MAKE THE TANGZHONG

1. Mix the flour and water in a small pan until smooth.
2. Place over high heat, stirring until the mixture begins to bubble and becomes thick.
3. Transfer to a bowl, cover the surface with cling film and leave to cool to room temperature or just warm.

TO MAKE THE DOUGH

1. Add all the ingredients for the dough into a mixing bowl with the tangzhong.
2. Mix with a table knife until it begins to form a dough, then squeeze the dough together in your hands.
3. Once it has become a single ball of dough with a couple of dry patches of flour, tip it onto a worktop.
4. Knead the dough for about 5–10 minutes. It will stop sticking to the table and will become far smoother through kneading, although it doesn't have to be completely smooth at the end.

5. Place back into the mixing bowl, cover with a tea towel or cling film and leave to prove for at least 30 minutes whilst you make the topping. It will rise and become smoother in this time.

MAKE THE TOPPING

1. Stir the butter and sugar until combined. Add in the flour and stir until fully combined.
2. If you want to colour the toppings, split the dough into as many portions as you want, from 1 to 6 (you can get 6 portions of 30g/1oz each from this mix). Add some gel food colour to each portion and stir through by pressing with the back of a spoon to achieve a vibrant colour.

SHAPE THE BUNS

1. Tip out the bread dough onto your worktop. Flatten the dough with your palms and cut it into 6 equal portions. You can weigh them if you like. Each should be about 90g (3¼oz).

2. Flatten one of the portions of dough. Stretch the edge of the dough at a point and pull it into the centre of the dough. Repeat this all around the dough and pinch all the folds together under the bun.

3. Flip the dough ball over so the seam is underneath the bun. Cup your hand over the bun, press down slightly and roll your hand around over the bun to create a smoother round shape.

4. Place the bun on a baking tray lined with baking paper and repeat the process for the rest of the dough to create 6 buns.

5. Lightly wet your hands for this stage to prevent the topping from sticking. Pick up one portion of the topping and press it in your palms into a flat round shape about the same size as the top of the bun. Lay it over one of the buns. Repeat this for the rest of the buns. It doesn't have to be a completely smooth round.

6. Use a small knife to cut squiggly lines into the topping on each bun. Don't cut the dough underneath.

7. Cover the buns lightly with cling film. Leave in a warm place to prove for 45 minutes–1 hour 30 minutes, until about doubled in size and very jiggly when you lightly shake the baking trays.

8. Preheat the oven to 170°C fan (375°F/gas 5) whilst the buns are proving. Once proved, bake the buns for about 20 minutes until the dough poking through under the coloured topping turns golden brown. Leave to cool before digging in alongside a hot chocolate!

BIRTHDAY BABKA

Babka is a sweet cake-like bread that originated in Jewish communities in Eastern Europe. 'Babka' means 'grandmother', and some say this name comes from the original tin that these cakes would be baked in, which would look a little like a skirt a grandmother might wear. Now, babkas are baked in many different shapes, most commonly in loaf tins. They can also be filled with lots of different things. The most common is probably chocolate. What all babkas do have in common is a very enriched dough (this means it has lots of butter and eggs in it) filled with a tasty filling that is rolled up tightly to give a swirly design in the bread. Because there is lots of butter and egg in this dough, it is almost closer to cake than bread.

I will be honest here, this is one of the most challenging bakes in the book. The dough gets quite long and can be tricky to handle and move. Try to be confident when you are handling the dough, and you can always grab a second pair of hands to help make braiding and moving the dough easier.

TIME REQUIRED

30 minutes prep
45 minutes chilling
1 hour proving
35 minutes baking

BAKING CHALLENGE

INGREDIENTS

For the dough

475g (1lb 1oz) plain flour

½ teaspoon salt

2 teaspoons fast-action dried yeast

30g (1oz) caster sugar

3 eggs

65ml (¼ cup) milk

1 teaspoon vanilla extract

100g (3½oz) butter, very soft

For the filling

225g (8oz) cream cheese

75g (2½oz) icing sugar

2 teaspoons vanilla extract

75g (2½oz) rainbow sprinkles

For the syrup

30g (1oz) sugar

2 tablespoons water

For the icing

50g (1¾oz) icing sugar

1½ teaspoons water

METHOD

MAKE THE DOUGH

1. Add the dough ingredients into a mixing bowl. Stir together with a table knife until it forms into a shaggy, rough dough.
2. Tip this out onto the work surface and knead for 5–10 minutes until combined into quite a smooth dough. It will be a little sticky at the start but shouldn't be once you're done kneading.
3. Place the dough back in the bowl, cover and leave in the fridge for at least 30 minutes.

MAKE THE FILLING

1. Sieve the icing sugar into the cream cheese. Add the vanilla and stir until combined.

ASSEMBLE, BAKE AND DECORATE THE BABKA

1. Remove the dough from the fridge and turn it out onto a lightly floured surface.
2. Press the dough flat with your palms and encourage it into a rough rectangle shape. Roll the dough into a rectangle about 50cm x 35cm (20" x 14").
3. Spread the cream cheese mixture over the filling in an even layer, leaving a border around the dough. Completely cover this cream cheese with rainbow sprinkles.
4. Roll the dough up into a tight spiral from one of the long ends.
5. Bend the roll of dough into a horseshoe shape and place it on a baking tray lined with baking paper. Cover the dough with cling film and chill the dough in the freezer for 15–30 minutes.
6. Unbend the dough and use a serrated knife to cut down the middle of the roll

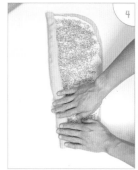

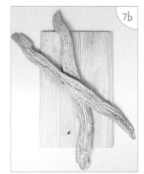
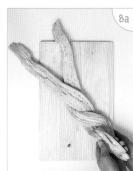

lengthways, chopping it into two long pieces.

7. Lay the two long pieces of dough next to each other with their cut sides facing up. Place the middle of one piece of dough over the middle of the other, creating a cross.

8. Twist the two pieces of dough around one another from the middle up and from the middle down, creating a braid. Keep the cut side of the babka facing up whilst you twist.

9. Wrap the long braided dough into a coil shape and tuck the end of the dough underneath the coil to hide it.

10. Pick up the coil and place it onto a baking tray lined with baking paper. Cover the dough lightly with clingfilm and place in a warm spot to prove for 45 minutes–1 hour 30 minutes until nearly doubled in size and puffy (this will take longer if you are working with very cold dough).

11. Whilst the dough is proving, preheat the oven to 160°C fan (350°F/gas 4). Bake the babka for about 35–40 minutes until golden all over.

12. Once the babka is out of the oven, add the sugar and water for the syrup into a pan and stir over high heat until the sugar has dissolved and the mixture bubbles.

13. Brush the syrup all over the warm babka to make it shiny. Throw some extra sprinkles over the babka whilst it is sticky with the syrup.

14. Once the babka is completely cool, mix the icing sugar with the water to make a thick but flowing icing. Drizzle this all over the babka from a height. Top with a few more sprinkles, and it's ready to serve.

Bake it your own

☆ You can use this recipe to make two loaf-shaped babkas. Once rolled up, slice the log in half lengthways. Slice and braid the two portions of dough as instructed in the main recipe, leaving them as a straight braid. Fill two greased and baking-paper-lined 900g (2lb) loaf tins with the doughs. Once proved, bake them for about 40 minutes.

☆ You can make a chocolate babka by replacing the cream cheese and icing sugar with 300g (10½oz) of chocolate spread. You can also keep the sprinkles or replace them with 75g (2½oz) chopped roasted hazelnuts.

LEMON ICED BUNS

An iced bun is a classic British bakery item. Sweet, soft, pillowy dough filled with a very generous serving of whipped cream makes this my dad's favourite item to pick up from the baker's. I have added lemon curd into the filling, which lends a little zing to the bake and helps prevent it from being overly rich or sweet, but you can use jam or your favourite toast topping instead.

Iced buns are typically baked in long finger shapes, but these can be pretty difficult to shape. Instead, I bake these as rounds in a baking tin, which is much easier to shape and leads to more evenly sized and shaped buns.

MAKES 12 BUNS

TIME REQUIRED
20 minutes prep
1 hour 30 minutes proving
20 minutes baking

BAKING CHALLENGE

INGREDIENTS

For the dough

600g (1lb 5oz) strong bread flour

1½ teaspoons salt

1 tablespoon fast-action dried yeast

60g (2oz) caster sugar

60g (2oz) butter, very soft

300ml (1¼ cup) milk

1 egg

For the filling

300ml (1¼ cup) double cream

30g (1oz) icing sugar

2 lemons, zest (optional)

250g (9oz) lemon curd

For the icing

200g (7oz) icing sugar

1 tablespoon + 2 teaspoons lemon juice

METHOD

MAKE THE DOUGH

1. Grease a 23cm x 33cm (9" x 13") tin and line the base with a sheet of baking paper.

2. Add all the dough ingredients into a bowl and stir until combined into a very rough, shaggy dough.

3. Tip this onto the worktop and knead for about 10 minutes until a lot less sticky and smoother. Place back in the bowl, cover with a tea towel and leave aside for at least 30 minutes to prove.

4. Tip out the dough onto your worktop. Flatten the dough with your palms and cut it into 12 equal portions. You can weigh them if you like; each should be about 90g (3¼oz). Cover the cut portions with a tea towel to prevent them from drying out.

5. Flatten one of the portions of dough. Stretch the edge of the dough at a point and pull it into the centre of the dough. Repeat this all around the dough and pinch all the folds together under the bun.

6. Flip the dough ball over so the seam is underneath the bun. Cup your hand over the bun, press down slightly and roll your hand around over the bun to create a smoother round shape.

7. Place this ball of dough into the lined tin in the corner. Repeat the shaping process with all of the portions of dough and fill the tin with 4 rows of 3 buns.

8. Cover the tin with a tea towel and sit in a warm place for 45 minutes–1 hour 30 minutes, until the buns have doubled in size, are touching one another and are jiggly when the tin is gently shaken.

9. Whilst the buns are proving, preheat the oven to 170°C fan (375°F/gas 5). Bake the proved buns for about 20 minutes until an even golden colour all over. Leave to cool in the tin.

FILL THE BUNS

1. Whisk the cream with the icing sugar and lemon zest (if using) until holding in soft peaks.

2. Tear apart the buns from one another. Split the cooled buns in half sideways. Spread a spoonful of lemon curd over the bottom piece of bun.

3. Spread a thick layer of cream over the lemon curd.

4. Top the cream with the top half of bun. Repeat this process for all the buns.

ICE THE BUNS

1. Add the icing sugar to a bowl and mix through the lemon juice until it is a very thick paste that can flow a little.

2. Pour a dessert spoonful of icing over the top of a bun and gently push it towards the edges. It looks nice when a couple of drips fall off the side. The icing will set after about 30 minutes.

Bake it your own

You can use any other spread as the filling for your buns. Jam is a classic, but you could use marmalade, other curds, or even go down a chocolate route.

BAKEWELL CRUFFINS

Cruffins are quite a recent invention in baking. They are a cross between a croissant and a muffin, hence the name 'cruffin'. Making croissant dough from scratch is one of the most challenging tasks in baking. It is a cross between a yeasted bread dough and a puff pastry that has layers of butter running through the dough. Bread doughs like warmth to rise, but puff pastry needs to be kept cold to keep the layers of butter and make a flaky pastry. Balancing these factors makes producing a light and flaky croissant with good layers challenging. I am not good enough at making croissants to tell you how to do it, so instead this recipe calls for shop-bought croissant dough, the type you get in tubes in a supermarket.

It's not cheating to use ready-made pastries and doughs. If it helps you to get baking, it's a good thing to use. However, it's nice to add something to it and make it your own when using these ready-made components. Here we fill the dough with frangipane (an almond cake batter) before rolling it up and baking it in a muffin tin. The result is quite far from what you might expect of a shop-bought croissant.

MAKES 6

TIME REQUIRED
20 minutes prep
20 minutes baking

BAKING CHALLENGE

INGREDIENTS

50g (1¾oz) butter, softened

50g (1¾oz) caster sugar

60g (2oz) ground almonds

1 egg

275–350g (10oz–12½oz) ready-made croissant dough

75g (2½oz) granulated sugar

50g (1¾oz) jam

METHOD

1. Preheat the oven to 170°C fan (375°F/gas 5). Grease 6 holes of a muffin tin.

2. Cream together the butter and sugar until combined. Mix through the almonds and egg and set aside.

3. Roll out the croissant dough on a well-floured surface to a width of 18cm (7") and quite long. It doesn't matter how long it is; the width is what's important. Some ready-made doughs come pre-cut into croissant shapes. Lay these all together into a single piece and roll them out together.

4. Use a palette knife to spread the filling over the croissant dough as evenly as possible.

5. Cut the dough into 6 x 3cm (1") wide strips that are very long. It is easiest to do this with a pizza cutter.

6. Roll up one of the strips and place it cut side down in the tin. Repeat this with the remaining strips of dough.

7. Bake for 20–25 minutes until deeply golden.

8. Leave to cool in the tin until cool enough to handle but still warm. Fill a bowl with the granulated sugar and roll a warm cruffin in the sugar to give it a sugary coating before leaving it to cool completely.

9. Cut an opening in the top of the cooled cruffins with a knife. Fill a piping bag with the jam and pipe some jam into the centre of each.

Bake it your own

You can substitute the jam filling for any other spreads. E.g. chocolate spread, caramel sauce, curds, marmalade.

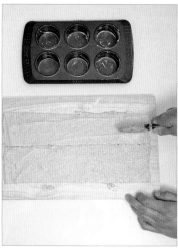
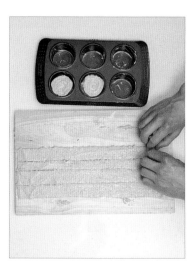

MONKEY BREAD

Monkey bread is all about being a little messy and uneven. It is made with random-sized little balls of sweet dough covered in butter and rolled in cinnamon sugar that are all randomly plonked into a tin with one another. They prove up and bake together to create a single loaf that you can pull apart like a tear and share. My favourite part of this bake is the bottom edge of the bread that sits in the corner of the tin. Lots of the butter and sugar sinks to the bottom of the tin whilst the dough is proving, and when it bakes, it turns super sticky and caramelly and all forms of awesome!

TIME REQUIRED
40 minutes prep
1 hour 30 minutes proving
40 minutes baking

BAKING CHALLENGE

INGREDIENTS

For the dough
425g (15oz) strong bread flour
2 teaspoons fast-action dried yeast
1 teaspoon salt
40g (1½oz) butter, very soft
40g (1½oz) caster sugar
200ml (¾ cup + 2 tablespoons) milk
1 egg

For the coating
100g (3½oz) butter
150g (5oz) light brown sugar
1 teaspoon ground cinnamon

METHOD

1. Grease and base line a deep 18cm (7") cake tin with baking paper.

2. Add all the dough ingredients to a bowl and stir with a table knife until it makes a rough, shaggy dough.

3. Tip this onto a worktop and knead for about 10 minutes until a lot less sticky and smoother. Place back into the bowl, cover and leave to prove for at least 30 minutes.

4. Melt the butter for the coating in a small bowl in the microwave. Leave to cool a little so it is still melted but not hot to the touch.

5. Split the 150g (5oz) of light brown sugar and 1 teaspoon of cinnamon between two separate bowls. You need two bowls of this to stop it from becoming too clumpy as you are coating the dough later.

6. Tip the proved dough out onto the worktop. Flatten with your palms and cut into 4 pieces.

7. Roll each quarter of the dough into a long log and cut about 10–15 pieces from each using a bench scraper to cut down on the dough. You don't need to be precise about the size of the dough pieces, they can be very rough.

8. Dip a ball of dough into the butter, let the excess butter drip off for a couple of seconds, then toss in the sugar and cinnamon mix before throwing into the lined tin, starting at the edge.

9. Repeat this process with the rest of the dough, filling up the tin. There can be gaps and spaces when adding the balls to the tin, but try to make the top fairly level when finished.

10. The brown sugar will get quite clumpy and thick as you work through the dough pieces. You can still coat the dough balls in this clumpy mixture, but once you have used up the first bowl of brown sugar, you can start fresh with the new bowl of brown sugar that isn't clumpy.

11. Once you have used all the dough, cover the tin with cling film and leave in a warm place to rise for 45 minutes–1 hour 30 minutes until about doubled in size, and sitting a little under the edge of the tin.

12. Whilst the dough is proving, preheat the oven to 160°C fan (350°F/gas 4). Bake for 40–45 minutes, and deeply golden and hard when tapped on top. Place a roasting tin under the cake tin in the oven to catch any dripping butter from the tin.

13. Leave to cool in the tin for about 10 minutes before running a knife around the edge of the tin and turning the loaf out whilst it is still warm. Be careful when dealing with the hot tin. You may need to ask for some help with this.

14. Leave to cool for at least 20 minutes before digging in. You can either slice it or tear apart the small buns. Eat warm or cold.

Bake it your own

You can make mini monkey breads by adding the balls of dough into a greased muffin tin. Fill the muffin tins half full before proving and baking for 15–20 minutes.

FILLED SWEET BAO

Bao buns are soft, steamed buns from China that can be filled or enjoyed plain. Steaming the buns gives them a pillowy texture with a slight chew around the outside. Bao can be stuffed with many different fillings, savoury or sweet. I am giving a list of ideas for sweet fillings, most of which aren't traditional at all but will be very tasty. You can also leave the buns unfilled if you like; this can be called Mantou. My flatmate, Claudia, is from Hong Kong and introduced me to a Chinese breakfast where you dip Mantou in condensed milk. It is delicious, and I think you should give it a try!

Filling ideas:

☆ Sweet red bean paste

☆ Chocolate hazelnut spread

☆ Peanut butter

☆ Biscoff spread

☆ Jam (must be a thick jam)

☆ Chocolate truffles

☆ No filling – after steaming, dip in condensed milk

MAKES 10 BUNS

TIME REQUIRED

40 minutes prep
1 hour resting/proving
15 minutes steaming

BAKING CHALLENGE

Bake it your own

I love savoury bao. There are fantastic recipes out there where you can find traditional and non-traditional filling ideas. For non-traditional savoury bao, you could fill them with the sweet potato bake filling from page 31.

INGREDIENTS

300g (10½oz) plain flour

2 teaspoons fast-action dried yeast

1 teaspoon caster sugar

1 tablespoon oil

140ml (½ cup + 1 tablespoon + 1 teaspoon) water

200g (7oz) filling (see suggestions above)

METHOD

1. Place the flour, yeast and sugar in a bowl. Add the oil and water and stir to combine.

2. Tip the mixture onto the work surface and knead the dough for about 10 minutes until it is a lot smoother. Place the dough back in the bowl, cover with a tea towel and set aside for 30 minutes. It should rise a little in this time and will become smoother.

3. Cut 10 small squares of baking paper about 5cm x 5cm (2" x 2").

4. Tip out the dough onto your worktop and flatten with your palms. Cut 10 portions from the dough. You can weigh the dough if you want; each should weigh about 40g (1½oz).

5. Flatten one of the portions of dough. Stretch the edge of

the dough at a point and pull it into the centre of the dough. Repeat this all around the dough and pinch all the folds together under the bun. Roll the dough between your hands into a rounder ball. Do this for all of the portions of dough and place them under a tea towel to stop them from drying out.

6. Take one ball of dough and roll it out to a rough circle with the seam side facing up. Roll out the edges thinner than the centre. Lift and turn the dough as you roll out the thin edges. The circle of dough should be about 10cm (4") in diameter.

7. Add a heaped tablespoon of filling (or a whole chocolate truffle) into the centre of the dough. Pull two opposite edges of the dough together over the filling, pinching them together. Repeat this at different parts of the dough until all of the filling has been covered up. Squeeze together all the seams of the dough.

8. Flip the ball of dough over so it is seam side down. Gently roll the ball of dough under a cupped hand to make it rounder, then lift the dough onto a piece of baking paper. If you have a steamer basket, place the bun in the basket now and cover. If you don't have a steamer basket, place on a plate and cover with a tea towel.

9. Repeat the shaping process with all the pieces of dough. Leave plenty of room between the bao buns when filling the basket, as they will grow much bigger when steaming. Leave the buns covered to prove for 15–30 minutes (you don't have to be very precise here).

10. If you have a steamer basket, fill your steamer pan or a wide pan with a couple of centimetres of water and bring to a gentle simmer. Place the steamer basket over the water, cover with the lid and steam for about 15 minutes.

11. Select a large pan with a lid if you do not have a steamer basket. Fill a cereal bowl with water and place in the bottom of the pan. Fill around the bowl with a couple of centimeters of water and bring to a gentle simmer. Place your bao buns on a plate that fits inside the pan, cover with a lid or tin foil and steam for about 15 minutes.

12. Remove the bao buns from the steamers using tongs and a fish slice and allow to cool for about 5 minutes before peeling off the baking paper underneath. You may need to steam the buns in two batches.

13. Enjoy the bao buns warm.

CHAPTER 4
NO-BAKES

Bake it your own

Try making a marble design. Melt 100g (3½oz) dark or milk chocolate and 50g (1¾oz) white chocolate in separate bowls, either in the microwave or over a pan of simmering water. Cover the traybake with the dark or milk chocolate, then drizzle the white chocolate over the top and with the tip of a table knife, gently swirl through the different chocolate colours to create a marble effect.

MALTESER SQUARES

GFO

Malteser squares were my favourite bake that my mum would make when I was in primary school. She picked up the recipe from a friend, who got it from a café in Northern Ireland, and now I am passing it on to you. I love the satisfying thick texture of the tiffin-like mixture with the crunch from the Maltesers and digestives. When the bake sits for a day or so, the Maltesers often soften and go a little chewy, which is awesome!

My mum would often make these for school or church bake sales. My brother and I would always beg her to leave some squares at home because we knew they would all sell out if they were taken to the bake sale!

MAKES 16 SQUARES

TIME REQUIRED
20 minutes prep
20 minutes chilling

BAKING CHALLENGE

INGREDIENTS

100g (3½oz) butter

60g (2oz) golden syrup

½ teaspoon salt

200g (7oz) digestive biscuits, roughly crushed

200g (7oz) Maltesers (plus an additional 20g/¾oz for decoration)

150g (5oz) chocolate (white, milk or dark)

Make this gluten-free

☆ Replace the digestives with gluten-free digestives.

☆ Replace the Maltesers with crushed-up Cadbury's Crunchie bars.

METHOD

1. Lightly grease a 20cm (8") square tin with oil and line the base and sides with baking paper.

2. Place the butter, syrup and salt over medium heat until the butter melts.

3. Roughly crush the digestives with your clean hands in a large mixing bowl. Add the Maltesers whole to the same bowl.

4. Pour the melted butter mix over the biscuits and Maltesers and mix well until the chocolate around the Maltesers has melted into the mixture and everything is well combined.

5. Firmly press the mixture into the lined tin using the back of a spoon.

6. Melt the chocolate in the microwave or in a bowl over a pan of simmering water, and pour over the mixture in the tin. Place 16 Malteser halves evenly spaced over the chocolate. Place in the fridge to set for at least 20 minutes, or until the chocolate has set.

7. Remove from the tin and slice into 16 squares.

ROCKY ROAD

You can't go into a café without finding they serve a rocky road. That's proof that everyone loves a rocky road! Considering how much people love it, it's ridiculously simple to prepare and takes so little time. And although simple to make, when eating a rocky road, you are hit with so many different textures, making it a really interesting bake to eat. Overall, it's one of the best bakes you can make for the effort involved.

MAKES 12 BARS

TIME REQUIRED
15 minutes prep
1 hour chilling

BAKING CHALLENGE

INGREDIENTS

300g (10½oz) milk chocolate

75g (2½oz) golden syrup

75g (2½oz) butter

½ teaspoon salt

85g (3oz) mini marshmallows

125g (4½oz) raisins

200g (7oz) shortbread, crushed

Icing sugar, for dusting

METHOD

1. Lightly grease and line a 20cm (8") square tin with baking paper overhanging the edges.
2. Add the chocolate, syrup, butter and salt to a bowl and melt in the microwave in 30-second bursts until fully melted (or in a bowl over a pan of simmering water).
3. Add the marshmallows, raisins and biscuits crushed into bitesized pieces to the melted chocolate mixture. Stir it all together until fully coated.
4. Tip this mixture into the prepared tin and level off with the back of a spoon. Leave in the fridge to set for at least 1 hour.
5. To release the rocky road from the tin, run a blunt knife between the baking paper and tin all around the bake, then pull it out using the baking paper.
6. Sieve over a generous dusting of icing sugar.
7. Cut the bake in half one way and then cut each half into 6 bars.

Bake it your own

✰ This is an entirely customisable bake. Feel free to use different biscuits to replace the shortbread and change the mix-ins of the raisins and marshmallows for nuts, sweeties, cereal, popcorn, other dried fruits or little chocolates. Anything goes!

✰ You can also use dark or white chocolate instead of milk chocolate.

Make this gluten-free

Replace the shortbread with a gluten-free biscuit.

HONEY NUTTY CEREAL SQUARES

GFO

These cereal squares are crunchy and sweet, but what makes them so moreish is that they have a wee salty hit. Salt acts as a flavour enhancer in baking and balances out very sugary bakes. You typically can't taste the salt, but the bake wouldn't taste as good without it. With the addition of salted peanuts in these squares, you do come across hits of salt, which, since this bake is full of super sweet marshmallows, is really needed.

MAKES 16 SQUARES

TIME REQUIRED
10 minutes prep
30 minutes chilling

BAKING CHALLENGE

INGREDIENTS

200g (7oz) marshmallows

50g (1¾oz) butter

½ teaspoon salt

160g (5½oz) honey nut cornflakes

100g (3½oz) bran flakes, lightly crushed

80g (2¾oz) salted peanuts

Make this gluten-free

Replace the cereals for gluten-free cereals.

Bake it your own

☆ Change the cereals used for your favourite flakes.

☆ Try using a different nut or something else with some crunch, like mini eggs.

METHOD

1. Line a 20cm (8") square tin with baking paper.

2. Add the marshmallows, butter and salt into a large microwave-safe bowl and heat on full power for about 2 minutes. Stir, then place back in for another minute.

3. Add the cereals and peanuts and stir until all covered in the sticky marshmallow mixture.

4. Pour this into the tin and press out into a flat layer. This is easiest done with the back of a lightly greased spoon to prevent it from sticking.

5. Leave to cool in the fridge for about 30 minutes or until firm enough to cut. Remove from the tin and cut into 16 squares.

GINGERBREAD POPCORN

GF

Paddington 2, Johnny English, *Cheaper by the Dozen*, *Moana*, *Kung Fu Panda* – all my favourite movies are made better when snacking on a bowl of popcorn during family movie night. But they are made even better when snacking on this popcorn! This takes hardly any time to prepare but leaves you with popcorn with the most amazing, crunchy-sweet exterior. It is so moreish and so good that it's hard to share with the person sitting next to you!

TIME REQUIRED
10 minutes

BAKING CHALLENGE

INGREDIENTS

50g (1¾oz) dark brown sugar

30g (1oz) golden syrup

30g (1oz) butter

½ teaspoon ground cinnamon

½ teaspoon ground ginger

¼ teaspoon mixed spice

½ teaspoon bicarbonate of soda

50g (1¾oz) salted popcorn

Bake it your own

You can remove the spices, and you will still make a deliciously crunchy, salty-sweet popcorn.

METHOD

1. Line a large, rimmed baking tray or roasting tin with baking paper.
2. Add the sugar, syrup, butter and spices into a big deep-sided pan over high heat, stirring until the butter has melted.
3. Once the mixture begins to bubble, leave it on the heat for 1 minute.
4. Throw in the bicarbonate of soda and stir, then add the popcorn off the heat and stir to coat all the popcorn. Be very careful as the mixture is incredibly hot!
5. Once the popcorn is coated in the mixture, pour it into the lined tin and spread out with a spoon into a flat layer.
6. Leave the mixture to cool and harden at room temperature before breaking up and enjoying.

COOKIE DOUGH TRUFFLES

GFO

Raw eggs and raw flour can be bad for us if eaten. This cookie dough doesn't have any eggs, and the flour is heated before being added. So, you can enjoy the taste of thick, stodgy cookie dough without any risks from uncooked flour and eggs. This is also amazing to mix into ice cream to make your own cookie dough flavour!

MAKES ABOUT 18 TRUFFLES

TIME REQUIRED
15 minutes

BAKING CHALLENGE

Make this gluten-free

☆ Replace the plain flour for gluten-free plain flour.

☆ Ensure your sprinkles are gluten free.

Bake it your own

You can substitute the chocolate chips for little fudge pieces or your favourite chocolates chopped up very small.

INGREDIENTS

125g (4½oz) plain flour
90g (3oz) butter, softened
100g (3½oz) light brown sugar
½ teaspoon salt
2 tablespoons milk
125g (4½oz) chocolate chips
50g (1¾oz) sprinkles (optional)

METHOD

1. Place the flour in a microwave-safe bowl and heat on full power for 30 seconds. Remove from the microwave and stir. Repeat this process three more times. This heats the flour and kills any bacteria that could be in it. Set aside to cool.

2. Cream together the butter, sugar and salt with an electric whisk for a couple of minutes until light and fluffy.

3. Mix through the cooled flour and milk to form a dough. Stir in the chocolate chips.

4. Scoop tablespoons of the dough and roll them into balls in the palm of your hand. Place on a baking tray.

5. Optional: roll the balls in sprinkles straight after scooping. They will firm up in the fridge, but I prefer eating them a little softer at room temperature.

CHOCOLATE MOUSSE PIE

GFO

This is quite a sophisticated dessert and will impress anyone who eats it. The crust is chocolatey and buttery, and it's filled with the most incredible light and airy chocolate mousse. For a chocolate lover, it's the perfect pudding!

Making a mousse is not the easiest process. Make sure you have three bowls ready to prepare the three separate components before combining them into a mousse. The most important part of making the mousse is to avoid overmixing once you have added to the final ⅔ of egg white. Once all the egg whites have been incorporated, continuing to mix will deflate the mix and make it heavy and dense, not light and airy.

The other tricky part about this is the shaping into a tart tin. You don't need to do this: you can just layer the biscuit base and mousse into individual ramekins or glasses. This will still be delicious but removes the jeopardy of turning out the full pie.

TIME REQUIRED

45 minutes prep
1 hour chilling

BAKING CHALLENGE

INGREDIENTS

For the biscuit base

250g (9oz) Bourbon biscuits

110g (4oz) butter

½ teaspoon salt

For the chocolate mousse

100g (3½oz) dark chocolate

100g (3½oz) milk chocolate

150ml (½ cup + 2 tablespoons) double cream

15g (½oz) icing sugar

120g (4¼oz) pasteurised egg white (3 large egg whites)

30g (1oz) caster sugar

For the topping (optional)

250g (9oz) chocolate sweets or berries

METHOD

MAKE THE BISCUIT BASE

1. Crush the biscuits into a crumb-like consistency in a food processor or by bashing them in a sealed bag with a rolling pin.

2. Melt the butter and stir this into the crushed biscuits with the salt.

3. Pour this mixture into a 20cm (8") loose-bottomed round tart tin. Firmly press it into all the corners and up the side of the tin using the bottom of a tumbler or mug. Place this in the fridge for at least 20 minutes until firm.

4. Carefully run a knife along the top edge of the tart tin to remove the excess crust overhanging.

FILL THE PIE

1. Melt the chocolate and leave it to cool for a couple of minutes until it is only slightly warm to the touch.
2. Whip the cream with the icing sugar until it just holds its shape.
3. Whisk the egg whites and sugar with an electric hand mixer until they form firm peaks.

4. Fold the melted but cooled chocolate into the whipped cream until nearly fully combined.
5. Add $\frac{1}{3}$ of the egg whites into the chocolate mixture and beat until fully combined. Then add the remaining $\frac{2}{3}$ of the egg whites and gently fold in with a flexible spatula until just combined. Pour this into the crust and set in the fridge for at least 1 hour to set.

ASSEMBLE AND SERVE

1. Before serving, gently warm the outside of the tart tin by blowing hot air from a hairdryer onto the side of the tin. Warming the sides of the tin melts the butter and allows it to slide out from the tin.
2. Top with chocolate sweets or berries if you want.

Make this gluten-free

Replace the bourbon biscuits for gluten-free chocolate sandwich biscuits.

Bake it your own

You can make the mousse as a stand-alone dessert. Fill ramekins with the mousse before setting them in the fridge.

SPECULOOS ICE BOX CAKE

GFO

The only components in this American-style cake are shop-bought biscuits layered with cream. It's not the standard way to make a cake, but trust me when I say you have to try it! The biscuits soften up as the cake sits in the fridge to the point where you can take a slice just like a sponge cake. None of my friends I tested this recipe on had tried this style of cake before, but they all loved it. For the people you feed this to, it's exciting and impressive. For you as the baker, it is beyond simple and very low effort to put together. A win-win!

I have chosen to use Speculoos biscuits for this cake. These are gorgeous little biscuits from Belgium with a caramelised and lightly cinnamon spiced taste. They are the biscuits I would always try to steal from the side of my parents' cups of coffee when out at a café. However, if you're not a fan of this biscuit, the good news is that you can still make this cake with any other biscuit you like.

TIME REQUIRED

30 minutes prep
3 hours chilling

BAKING CHALLENGE

INGREDIENTS

150g (5oz) mascarpone

300ml (1¼ cups) double cream

50g (1¾oz) dark brown sugar

Approx. 550g (1lb 4oz) or
  70 Speculoos biscuits

METHOD

1. With an electric whisk, whip the mascarpone with the cream and sugar until it is soft but holds its shape when the whisk is removed from the bowl.

2. Arrange six biscuits on your serving plate in a hexagon shape. Secure these to the plate with a dod of cream under each biscuit.

3. Fill the centre of the hexagon with three more biscuits arranged in a triangle and break another biscuit to fill the centre of the triangle. Secure these biscuits to the plate with a dod of cream under each one.

4. Top the biscuits with a large spoon of the cream (you want to use about $\frac{1}{7}$ of the cream mixture, or about 75g/2½oz). Spread this out into an even thin layer using a palette knife, leaving a small border of uncovered biscuits.

5. Top this layer of cream with another layer of biscuits in the same pattern as before, but offset the biscuits from

Bake it your own

Use your favourite shop-bought biscuits to build this cake. Some good ones would be digestives, malted milks, Bourbons, custard creams and Oaties.

Make this gluten-free

Use your favourite gluten free biscuits to build the cake.

the layer below so the middle of the sides of the top hexagon are sitting over the corners of the lower hexagon.

6. Repeat this so you have seven layers of biscuits (or as many as you like, you can easily make this cake smaller). Spread the remaining cream over the top of the final layer. Crumble a biscuit over the top of the cake.

7. Place the cake in the fridge overnight (or at least 3 hours) to allow the biscuits to soften before slicing and serving.

BISCUITS & COOKIES

COOKIE CAKE

If you've ever been disappointed when you finish a chocolate chip cookie too quickly, this is the bake for you. This is a mega-sized chocolate chip cookie with crisp edges and a seriously thick, chewy centre. A giant cookie also needs some giant chocolate chunks. I just break chocolate bars into their squares a mix these through the cookie dough. You can also use this recipe to make regular-sized cookies (see the 'Bake it your own' box), which are just as delicious, although not quite as showstopping.

TIME REQUIRED

15 minutes prep
30 minutes baking

BAKING CHALLENGE

INGREDIENTS

150g (5¼oz) butter

80g (2¾oz) caster sugar

100g (3½oz) light brown sugar

½ teaspoon salt

1 egg

210g (7½oz) plain flour

½ teaspoon bicarbonate of soda

200g (7oz) chocolate, broken into big chunks

Make this gluten-free

Replace the plain flour with gluten-free plain flour and ¼ teaspoon xanthan gum.

METHOD

1. Preheat the oven to 160°C fan (350°F/gas 4). Grease and base line a 20cm (8") round tin (preferably loose-bottomed) with baking paper.

2. Melt the butter in the microwave or a pan. Add this to a mixing bowl with the caster sugar, light brown sugar and salt. Whisk to combine. Crack the egg into the mixture and whisk.

3. Add the flour and bicarbonate of soda and stir with a spatula until combined into a thick cookie dough. Throw in 125g (4½oz) of the chocolate chunks and stir to incorporate.

4. Spoon the dough into the tin and use the back of a spoon to flatten it out. Press the remaining chocolate chunks into the dough from the top.

5. Bake in the oven for 30–35 minutes until it has a slight wobble in the middle of the cookie. Leave to completely cool to room temperature in the tin.

6. Carefully run a knife around the outside and turn the cooled cookie out like a cake. This is easier if it is a loose-bottomed tin where you can push the cookie out.

7. Cut the cookie into slices like a pizza. Eat cold on its own or serve warm with a scoop of ice cream melting into it.

Bake it your own

Make individual cookies by chilling the dough for 30 minutes. Then portion out 10 balls of cookie dough; each should weigh about 80g (2¾oz). Give lots of space between the cookies so they can spread. Bake them at 160°C fan (350°F/gas 4) for 15–17 minutes until deep golden around the edges and light golden in the centre.

CHOCOLATE CRINKLE COOKIES

GFO

These cookies have an amazing texture. They puff up in the oven as they bake, then sink back down a little as they cool, giving them their crinkly appearance and name. This creates a crispy edge around the cookie and a great chew in the centre. The cookies are rolled in granulated sugar and icing sugar, making a patchy black and white design on top, so you don't need to do any decoration once they are out of the oven. They already look beautiful!

MAKES 18–20 COOKIES

TIME REQUIRED
10 minutes prep
1 hour chilling
15 minutes baking

BAKING CHALLENGE

INGREDIENTS

100g (3½oz) butter

90g (3¼oz) caster sugar

90g (3¼oz) light brown sugar

½ teaspoon salt

1 egg

50g (1¾oz) cocoa powder

100g (3½oz) plain flour

½ teaspoon baking powder

35g (1½oz) granulated sugar

60g (2oz) icing sugar

METHOD

1. Preheat the oven to 160°C fan (350°F/gas 4). Line two baking trays with baking paper.

2. Melt the butter in a pan over medium heat or in the microwave. Pour this into a mixing bowl and whisk in the caster sugar, light brown sugar and salt. Add the egg and whisk through.

3. Sieve over the cocoa powder, plain flour and baking powder and use a spatula to stir through into a thick dough. Chill in the fridge for at least 1 hour. If you are in a rush, you can put it in the freezer for 30 minutes. It will firm up in the fridge/freezer and become workable.

4. Add the granulated sugar and icing sugar into two separate bowls. Roll tablespoon-sized balls of dough, then roll these in the granulated sugar to pick up a thin layer. Dunk these into the bowl of icing sugar and toss around to cover in a thick layer.

5. Place the balls well spread apart on the baking trays and bake for 12–15 minutes. The outside edge should feel slightly firm, but the cookie will be incredibly soft. Leave to cool completely on the baking trays.

Bake it your own

Try sandwiching two cookies together with caramel, jam, marshmallow fluff, or another filling.

Make this gluten-free

Replace the plain flour with gluten-free plain flour and ¼ teaspoon xanthan gum.

STUFFED PEANUT BUTTER COOKIES

This bake is at danger of being over the top. It isn't dainty or pretty, but it is very, very tasty. A satisfyingly thick peanut butter cookie filled with a soft gooey centre. There is so much peanut butter in this cookie dough, so it has a big peanut butter flavour, and it also adds to the chew of the cookie.

You can eat these warm when the fillings will be soft and oozing (and it will be pretty messy to eat!), or you can leave them to cool, and they will become firmer and chewier. If you fancy an indulgent pudding of hot cookie and ice cream, you can reheat the cookies in the microwave for 15–20 seconds.

MAKES 10 COOKIES

TIME REQUIRED
1 hour chilling
30 minutes prep
15 minutes baking

BAKING CHALLENGE

INGREDIENTS

For the filling
10 tablespoons chocolate hazelnut spread or peanut butter; or
10 marshmallows and 10 squares of chocolate

For the cookie dough
300g (10½oz) light brown sugar
300g (10½oz) peanut butter
1½ teaspoons bicarbonate of soda
½ teaspoon salt
2 eggs
50g (1¾oz) plain flour
150g (5¼oz) chocolate chips

METHOD

1. If filling the cookies with chocolate hazelnut spread or peanut butter: measure out 10 tablespoon measures on a lined baking tray and freeze them for at least 1 hour before making the dough.

2. Preheat the oven to 160°C fan (350°F/gas 4). Line two baking trays with baking paper.

3. Add the sugar, peanut butter, bicarbonate of soda, salt and eggs into a bowl and mix with an electric whisk until combined.

4. Stir through the flour, followed by the chocolate chips.

5. Split the dough into 10 portions. This is easiest if you weigh each ball of dough with electric scales. Each ball should be about 90g (3¼oz).

6. Flatten each ball of dough into a disc.

7. Fill the flattened discs with a frozen chocolate hazelnut spread or peanut butter tablespoon or a marshmallow and a square of chocolate.

8. Wrap the cookie dough around the fillings, so they are completely covered with the cookie dough.

9. Place the filled cookies on the baking trays, leaving a lot of room between them for spreading (you may need to bake in two batches). Press down on them slightly and bake for 15–17 minutes and golden around the edges (if you like a crunchy cookie, bake them longer, if you like a soft cookie, bake them less).

10. Leave to cool on the tray for at least 10 minutes before eating warm or cold after further cooling.

11. The filling will firm up as the cookie cools. You can reheat and soften the cookie later by popping it in the microwave for 15–20 seconds.

Bake it your own

You can bake these cookies without the fillings. They will bake in about the same time at the same temperature as the filled cookies.

Make this gluten-free

Replace the plain flour with gluten-free plain flour.

RAINBOW SWIRLS

Rainbowy, swirly and biscuity. These cookies are simple in flavour but striking in design. The near hypnotising rainbow swirls look complicated, but they're actually quite simple to make.

Make sure you chill the cookies well before baking and slicing to make it easier to get clean cuts.

MAKES 24–30 BISCUITS

TIME REQUIRED

40 minutes prep
20 minutes chilling
10 minutes baking

BAKING CHALLENGE

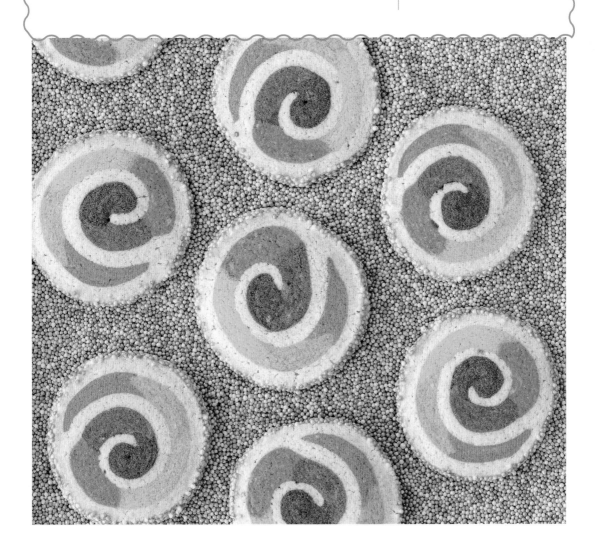

INGREDIENTS

200g (7oz) butter, softened

125g (4½oz) caster sugar

1 egg

1 teaspoon vanilla extract

½ teaspoon salt

350g (12½oz) plain flour

Red, orange, yellow, green, blue and purple gel food colours

1 egg white

50g (1¾oz) rainbow sprinkles

METHOD

1. Preheat the oven to 160°C fan (350°F/gas 4). Line two baking trays with baking paper.

2. Cream the butter and sugar with an electric whisk until light and fluffy.

3. Stir through the remaining ingredients – except the colours, egg white and sprinkles – until the mixture begins to form clumps. Use your hands to press and gently knead the mixture into a ball of dough.

4. Split the dough into two portions. Roll one piece of dough out between two sheets of baking paper in a rough rectangle about 26cm x 22cm (10" x 8½").

5. Split the second portion of dough into six pieces. Add one colour of gel food colouring to each piece and work through with your hands over a sheet of baking paper to have a rainbow of doughs. Wash your hands quickly after using the colours, so you don't have stained rainbow hands for days!

6. Roll each portion of dough into a log a couple of centimetres shorter than the length of the plain dough rectangle.

7. Remove the top layer of baking paper from the plain dough and lay the rainbow logs as shown in photo 7a over the dough. Flatten them slightly with your hands.

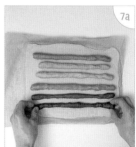
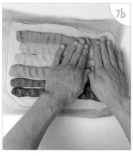

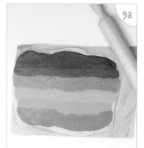

8. Place a sheet of baking paper over the dough and roll out until the coloured dough reaches the edges of the plain dough.

9. Remove the top layer of paper from the dough. Roll the dough into a tight spiral from one of the long sides. If the dough gets stuck to the paper, place it in the fridge for 3–5 minutes before trying again.

10. Brush the outside of the log with a light layer of egg white and roll it in the rainbow sprinkles. Wrap in baking paper and leave it in the fridge for at least 20 minutes to firm up.

11. Cut ½–¾cm (¼–⅓") slices from the dough. Place on baking trays with a bit of space between them and bake for 10–12 minutes or until they are browning a little on the top edges. Allow to cool completely on the baking trays. They will firm up as they cool.

Make this gluten-free

☆ Replace the plain flour with gluten-free plain flour and ½ teaspoon xanthan gum.

☆ Ensure the sprinkles you use are gluten-free.

Bake it your own

☆ Make polka-dot and rainbow marble cookies:

  ☆ Press tiny balls of coloured dough onto the rolled out plain dough. Briefly roll again and use a cookie cutter to cut polka dot biscuits from the dough.

  ☆ Lightly knead the leftover dough. Roll it into a log and chill, then slice and bake as instructed above to create rainbow marble cookies.

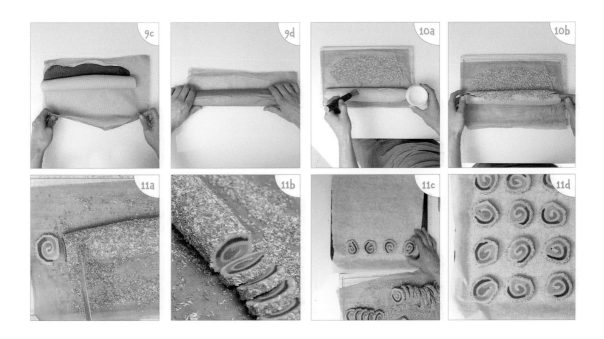

CHOCOLATE ORANGE THUMBPRINT COOKIES

These biscuits are very "short". That is the term used to describe crumbly and soft bakes that don't have much chew. It refers to the dough's gluten network, which can either be short (like in biscuits and cakes) or long (like in bread).

These biscuits are short because they have lots of butter and some cornflour in them. The classic orange chocolate flavour and delightfully soft and crumbly "short" texture make these small biccies very moreish!

MAKES ABOUT 20 BISCUITS

TIME REQUIRED
30 minutes prep
15 minutes baking

BAKING CHALLENGE

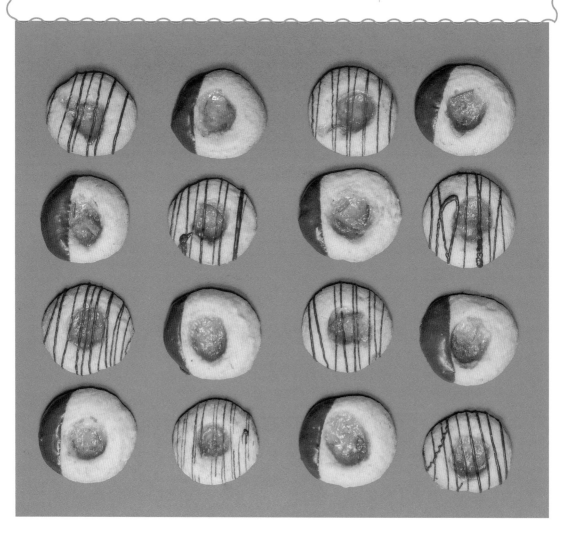

INGREDIENTS

For the biscuits

200g (7oz) butter, softened

50g (1¾oz) icing sugar

½ teaspoon salt

200g (7oz) plain flour

30g (1oz) cornflour

1 teaspoon orange extract

Zest of 1 large orange

1 tablespoon milk

For the filling

75g (2½oz) marmalade

100g (3½oz) orange flavoured chocolate

Make this gluten-free

Replace the plain flour with gluten-free plain flour and ¼ teaspoon xanthan gum.

Bake it your own

You can bake these cookies with different fillings instead of marmalade. You can use jam, curd, chocolate spread, caramel, or anything else to fill the biscuits' divot. If you use a different filling, you might want to remove the orange zest and extract from the biscuits and use a different chocolate to finish them off.

METHOD

1. Preheat the oven to 170°C fan (375°F/gas 5). Line two baking trays with baking paper.

2. Cream the butter until light and fluffy. Add the icing sugar and salt, and beat on high speed until combined.

3. Add in all the remaining biscuit ingredients and mix with an electric whisk until combined into a soft dough.

4. Scrape out portions of the dough using a tablespoon measure and roll into a ball in the palm of your hands. Place the balls well spread out on the baking trays. You should get about 20 from this mixture.

5. Press your thumb down into the centre of each ball to create a small divot. Fill each divot with ½ teaspoon marmalade.

6. Bake the biscuits for 13–15 minutes, or until they are picking up a light golden colour around the edges. Leave to cool on the tray. They will be very soft out of the oven but will firm up as they cool.

7. Melt the chocolate in the microwave or in a bowl over simmering water. Pour this into a deep mug or glass and dip one half of each cooled biscuit into the chocolate. Place back onto the baking tray and leave at room temperature until the chocolate has set or for 20 minutes before placing in the fridge to set. Alternatively, you can drizzle the chocolate over the cookies with a spoon from a height.

CRANBERRY & PISTACHIO FLORENTINES

GFO

Florentines are little biscuits made of a caramel-like mixture combined with lots of nuts and dried fruit. This recipe makes Florentines that are very snappy and crisp. They taste delicious. However, their crispy-thin texture also means they are at risk of breaking when you move them about, so do handle them with care. They are fragile!

MAKES 12 FLORENTINES

TIME REQUIRED
20 minutes prep
15 minutes baking

BAKING CHALLENGE

Bake it your own

☆ You can switch out the cranberries and pistachios for your favourite dried fruit and nuts.

☆ Once the Florentines are baked, you can use different shapes of cookie cutters to cut out shaped Florentines.

Make this gluten-free

Replace the plain flour with gluten-free plain flour.

INGREDIENTS

For the Florentines

60g (2oz) butter

40g (1½oz) caster sugar

40g (1½oz) light brown sugar

20g (¾oz) plain flour

Pinch of salt

50g (1¾oz) dried cranberries

50g (1¾oz) flaked almonds

30g (1oz) pistachios, roughly chopped

For decoration

30g (1oz) white chocolate

METHOD

1. Preheat the oven to 180°C fan (400°F/gas 6). Line two baking trays with baking paper.

2. Melt the butter, caster sugar and light brown sugar in a pan over medium heat.

3. Once melted, pour into a mixing bowl and stir through the flour and a pinch of salt. Add all the remaining Florentine ingredients and mix until all evenly coated and combined into a rough crumbly mixture.

4. Spoon 6 tablespoons of mixture onto each baking tray, well spread apart. Spread out the crumbly mounds into a flat round shape. It won't be a single mass of dough; it will be a crumbly mix spread out. Bake in the oven for 10–12 minutes and deep golden all over. Leave to cool completely on the baking trays.

5. If you want to make super neat Florentines, use a cookie cutter to cut the baked Florentines 2 minutes after they're out of the oven.

6. Flip the cooled Florentines upside down. Melt the white chocolate in a bowl over a pan of simmering water or in the microwave, and drizzle the melted white chocolate over the Florentines with a spoon.

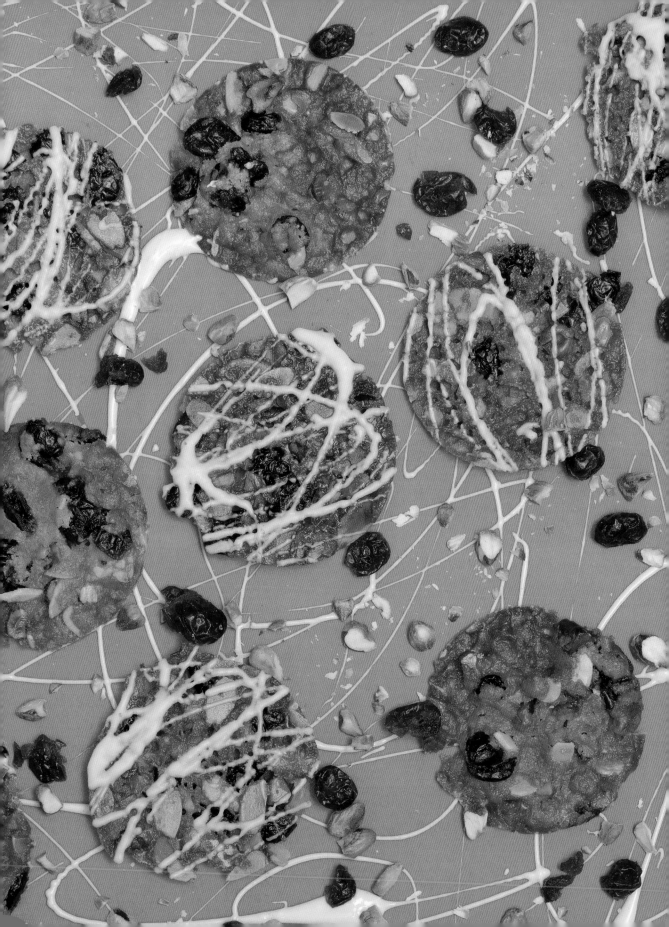

MILLIONAIRE'S CORONATION SLICE

GFO

This is a twist on a classic millionaire's shortbread. Instead of shortbread, the base is made with a bake my gran and mum made when we were young called Coronation Slice, a crunchy traybake made with cornflakes and coconut. There is a recipe for this bake in my first book, *Peter Bakes*. This is one of my all-time favourite recipes from my mum. But I had the thought that adding caramel and chocolate surely couldn't make this worse. I was right. Adding caramel and chocolate and turning this recipe into a "Millionaire's Coronation Slice" was a good move!

Make sure you bake the base to quite a dark brown: this will ensure it is nicely crisp and contrasts with the texture of the soft caramel sitting on top.

MAKES 25 SQUARES

TIME REQUIRED
30 minutes prep
20 minutes baking
2+ hours chilling

BAKING CHALLENGE

INGREDIENTS

For the base
80g (2¾oz) cornflakes
130g (4½oz) self-raising flour
80g (2¾oz) desiccated coconut
80g (2¾oz) caster sugar
½ teaspoon salt
100g (3½oz) butter

For the caramel
180g (6½oz) butter
120g (4¼oz) dark brown sugar
30g (1oz) golden syrup
½ teaspoon salt
1 tin condensed milk (397g/14oz)

For the topping
200g (7oz) milk chocolate
Extra cornflakes and desiccated coconut

Make this gluten-free

☆ Replace the cornflakes in the base with gluten-free cornflakes.

☆ Replace the self-raising flour in the base for gluten-free self-raising flour.

METHOD

1. Preheat the oven to 170°C fan (375°F/ gas 5). Line a 20cm (8") square tin with baking paper.

MAKE THE BASE

1. Roughly crush the cornflakes with your hands, then mix with the flour, coconut, sugar and salt in a large bowl.

2. Melt the butter and pour over the dry ingredients. Stir until everything is evenly coated with butter.

3. Tightly pack this mixture into a flat layer in the tin with the back of a spoon. Bake for 20 minutes. It should be deep golden on the surface. Leave aside to cool in the tin.

MAKE THE CARAMEL

1. Add all the caramel ingredients, except the condensed milk, into a pan over low heat, stirring until the butter has melted and the sugar has dissolved.

2. Add in the condensed milk, increase the heat to medium-high and bring to a simmer. Cook the bubbling mixture for 2–3 minutes, frequently stirring to stop it burning. This mixture gets very hot, so make sure to grab some help if needed.

3. Pour this mixture over the base and chill in the fridge for about 2 hours, or until the caramel is quite firm and cool to the touch.

TOP THE SQUARES

1. Melt the chocolate. Pour this over the cooled caramel and spread it into an even layer with a palette knife.

2. Sprinkle some cornflakes and coconut over the chocolate, then leave to set in the fridge for about 20 minutes until set. Cut into 20–25 portions.

SUGAR COOKIES

I have designed this recipe to be a basic go-to recipe for anytime you want to make simple biscuits that you can decorate. This makes buttery sweet biscuits that are very simple in flavour but very enjoyable to eat. I have also provided recipes for royal icing and water icing, and basic guidance on how you can pipe icing and dip ice biscuits.

I do hope, however, that you can use this recipe as a base from which you can explore your own creative ideas for decoration. You can cut the biscuits into any shape with a stencil or a cookie cutter. Ice the biscuits with any colours, in any design, using any additional toppings you like. Often, if you have a decoration idea for a biscuit, it can be good to do a Google or YouTube search to get inspiration on how you can use icing and decoration to get the design result you are looking for. You can also just have fun with it. Whether you are trying to recreate an image or character, or if you are just throwing colour and shapes at it, the main goal is just to have fun!

MAKES 16–20 BISCUITS

TIME REQUIRED

15 minutes prep
20 minutes chilling
15 minutes baking
1+ hour decorating

BAKING CHALLENGE

INGREDIENTS

For the biscuits

100g (3½oz) butter

65g (2¼oz) caster sugar

1 egg yolk

1 teaspoon vanilla extract

Pinch of salt

175g (6¼oz) plain flour

For the royal icing (for piping)

40g (1½oz) pasteurised egg white

1 teaspoon lemon juice

240g (8½oz) icing sugar

1 tablespoon water

Gel food colours

For the water icing (for dipping)

150g (5¼oz) icing sugar

1 tablespoon + 1 teaspoon water

Gel food colours

Make this gluten-free

Replace the plain flour in the biscuits with gluten-free plain flour and ¼ teaspoon xanthan gum.

METHOD

MAKE THE BISCUITS

1. Preheat the oven to 160°C fan (350°F/gas 4).

2. Cream the butter and sugar with an electric mixer until light and fluffy (3–5 minutes).

3. Stir through the remaining biscuit ingredients until the mixture begins to form clumps. Use your hands to press and gently knead the mixture into a ball of dough.

4. Place the dough between two sheets of baking paper. Roll it out to a little less than ½cm (¼") thick. Place this in the fridge for at least 15 minutes to firm up.

5. Remove the dough from the fridge and cut out shapes from the dough using any shape of cookie cutter you like.

6. Briefly knead together and re-roll the leftover pieces of dough between baking paper and cut out more shapes. If the dough gets too soft to handle, place it back in the fridge for 10 minutes until firm enough to cut.

7. Use the sheets of paper used for rolling to line two baking trays. Place your cookies on the baking trays and bake for 10–12 minutes until lightly browning around the edges. Remove from the oven and leave to cool on the baking trays before moving.

MAKE THE ROYAL ICING AND PIPE DECORATION

1. Add the egg white, lemon juice and icing sugar to a mixing bowl. Whisk with an electric mixer for a couple of minutes. It should be a smooth consistency that slowly falls off a spoon in large clumps. If it's too thick and doesn't fall off a spoon, add in a tiny bit of water (¼ teaspoon at a time). If it is too thin, add in more icing sugar, about 1 tablespoon at a time.

2. Split the icing at this stage and colour different portions with gel colouring. Cover any royal icing not being used immediately with a layer of cling film to prevent it from drying out.

3. Fill a piping bag with the icing you will use for the

main colour. Cut a tiny hole into the bag and pipe a thin line of icing around the border of all the cookies.

4. Pipe out the rest of the icing into a bowl, and add about 1 tablespoon of water to this icing to make it thinner, so it runs off a spoon in a slow, smooth flow.

5. Spoon the thinner icing over the biscuits and use the back of a spoon to push the icing towards the piped border of the biscuits. The border will stop the icing from dripping over the edge.

6. Top with sweets and sprinkles whilst the icing is soft. Leave the biscuits for about 30 minutes uncovered for the icing to set a little, then pipe over any more decorations with different colours of royal icing.

MAKE THE WATER ICING AND DIP DECORATE

1. Add the icing sugar and water to a bowl, and mix to combine. The mixture should coat the back of a spoon and drizzle in a thick, relatively slow flow.

2. Colour the icing with gel food colouring at this stage if you want.

3. Carefully hold a biscuit by the sides. Dip the top of the biscuit into a bowl of icing. Lift it out from the icing and shake it gently to encourage excess icing to fall off for about 15 seconds. Turn the biscuits over and leave for at least 1 hour for the icing to set.

4. If some of the icing drips down the side of the biscuits, after 15 minutes of setting, run a piece of kitchen roll around the edge of the biscuits to scrape away the dripping icing.

USE WATER ICING TO MAKE A MARBLE COOKIE DESIGN

1. Take ¼ of the icing from the bowl and colour this portion (you can also try splitting the small portion of icing into more bowls and using many different colours).

2. Drizzle some of the coloured portions of icing over the white icing and run a toothpick through the icing a couple of times to create a ripple.

3. Dip the biscuits, as instructed above, to reveal a marble icing design.

Bake it your own

Go all out with decoration! I don't want to lead you down a specific line. Think of a design, decide what colours you need and go for it! You can make it look like something or just throw sweets and sprinkles at it!

CHAPTER 6

CAKE

LEMON & BLUEBERRY DRIZZLE

Lemon drizzle cake is a huge crowd-pleaser, but it's a cake I feel is often forgotten about. The sharp zesty flavour of lemon is brilliant for cakes because it cuts through the rich sweet sponge made with lots of butter and sugar. The drizzle component of this cake comes from a simple syrup made by mixing lemon juice with sugar which is drizzled over the cake after it comes out of the oven. The lemon juice will sink into the sponge and help it stay extra moist, and the sugar will sit on top of the sponge, creating a crunchy top which is my favourite part of a slice of this cake. It's best to use granulated sugar for the drizzle, but you can use caster sugar if that is all you have.

Blueberries pair so well with lemon. They look like little jewels floating in the sponge when you slice into this loaf. When you eat one in the cake, it's a little pop of freshness and sweetness. However, if you're not a fan of blueberries or don't love the texture in the cake, you can still make a delicious lemon drizzle without the blueberries.

GFO

TIME REQUIRED

20 minutes prep
1 hour baking

BAKING CHALLENGE

INGREDIENTS

For the cake

175g (6oz) butter, softened

175g (6oz) caster sugar

½ teaspoon salt

2 lemons, zest

1 teaspoon lemon extract (optional)

200g (7oz) self-raising flour

3 eggs

100g (3½oz) blueberries

For the drizzle

100g (3½oz) granulated sugar

1 lemon, juice

METHOD

1. Preheat the oven to 160°C fan (350°F/gas 4). Grease a 900g (2lb) loaf tin with butter. Line the base and long sides of the tin with a single long piece of baking paper overhanging the sides.

2. Cream the butter, sugar, salt and lemon zest with an electric hand whisk until light and fluffy. Add the lemon extract, if using.

3. Add the flour and eggs and mix until just combined into a thick batter.

4. Fill the tin with half of the batter and spread it flat with the back of a spoon. Sprinkle over half of the blueberries and top this with the rest of the batter. Level off the top of the cake and sprinkle over the remaining blueberries.

5. Bake for 50–60 minutes or until a skewer comes out

Bake it your own

You can switch out the lemons for a different citrus fruit. Try oranges, limes or grapefruit.

Make this gluten-free

Replace the self-raising flour in the cake with gluten-free self-raising flour plus ¼ teaspoon xanthan gum.

clean when inserted into the centre of the cake. (Loaf tin shapes can vary – my one is short and deep. If you have a long loaf tin, it might take about 15 minutes less to bake.)

6. When the cake is just out of the oven, mix the granulated sugar for the drizzle with the juice of a lemon into a grainy mix. Spoon this over the top of the cake, spreading out any sugary clumps over the surface of the cake. The lemon juice will soak into the sponge as the cake cools, and the sugar will leave a crunchy top.

7. Once completely cool, remove the cake from the tin.

STP MUFFINS

I know people will ask me what my favourite recipe from this book is. I will probably switch between many different answers because I love every recipe in this book. However, this recipe has a very good shot at being my favourite. It is inspired by my favourite pudding of all: the Sticky Toffee Pudding. I love a hot moist sponge with lashings of toffee sauce and ice cream. However, you can't take a hot sticky toffee pudding on the move; it's very messy to eat! These muffins are a solution so you can eat the flavours of a sticky toffee pudding without needing a spoon.

The sponge is incredibly moist, rich and caramelly. This is in large part due to the dates in the batter. If you don't love dried fruit in cakes, don't worry. You can't feel the texture of the dates in the final cake. They are broken down by being soaked in water and bicarbonate of soda. They help make the cake incredibly moist and sticky and give it a great caramelly flavour.

If you're a sticky toffee fan, like me, I hope you love these muffins as much as I do!

MAKES 10 MUFFINS

TIME REQUIRED
30 minutes prep
20 minutes baking

BAKING CHALLENGE

INGREDIENTS

For the cake

150g (5oz) dates, cut small with scissors

½ teaspoon bicarbonate of soda

½ teaspoon salt

150ml (½ cup + 2 tablespoons) boiling water

100g (3½oz) butter, softened

115g (4oz) dark brown sugar

2 eggs

150g (5oz) self-raising flour

75g (2½oz) pecans, chopped (optional)

For the sauce

75g (2½oz) dark brown sugar

15g (½oz) butter

50ml (3 tablespoons + 1 teaspoon) double cream

¼ teaspoons salt

For the topping

200ml (¾ cup + 2 tablespoons) double cream

20g (¾oz) dark brown sugar

Extra pecans for decoration

Bake it your own

☆ Make the full-on pudding version of these muffins:

    ☆ Bake the muffins as instructed and remove them from their cases.

    ☆ Multiply all the sauce ingredients by three to make more sauce to serve with the puddings.

    ☆ Serve the pudding and sauce hot with ice cream. If you prepare the sauce and puddings ahead of time, you can reheat the puddings in the microwave for 30–90 seconds and reheat the sauce gently in a pan on the hob.

Make this gluten-free

Replace the self-raising flour with gluten-free self-raising flour.

METHOD

1. Preheat the oven to 170ºC fan (375ºF/gas 5). Fill a muffin tin with 10 muffin cases.
2. Add the dates, bicarbonate soda and salt into a bowl and pour over the boiling water. Leave this to stand for 15 minutes.
3. Cream together the butter and sugar until light and fluffy. Mix through the eggs, flour, pecans (if using) and soaked dates with their liquid.
4. Fill the 10 muffin cases about two-thirds full. Bake in the oven for about 20 minutes and a skewer inserted into the centre comes out clean.

MAKE THE SAUCE

1. Heat all the sauce ingredients over medium heat, stirring until the butter has melted and the sugar has dissolved, making a smooth sauce.
2. Set aside and leave to cool in the fridge. Once cool, fill a piping bag with the sauce.

ASSEMBLE THE CUPCAKES

1. Whip the cream with the dark brown sugar until it's just firm enough to hold its shape.
2. Press the sauce-filled piping bag into the centre of a muffin and squeeze some sauce into the centre of the cake. Alternatively, you can poke the top of the cakes with a skewer and drizzle over a teaspoon of the sauce whilst it is still warm.
3. Spoon a mound of whipped cream onto the muffins. Top with a pecan half and drizzle over some of the remaining cooled sauce from a height.

BLONDIES

Blondies are just like brownies without chocolate, so they look blonde instead of brown. Blondie recipes have been around longer than brownie recipes, although brownies are much more common than their butterscotch-tasting cousin now.

These blondies are seriously fudgy. The centre piece is basically just fudge with a crispy top! The outside pieces have a firmer, more biscuity texture around the very edge and become fudgier the further in you go. I like to place chunks of chocolate over the base of the tin, which caramelise and go golden and crispy on the bottom when baked. The fudgy texture, deep butterscotch flavour and big chocolate chunks make this delicious but also very rich, so I strongly advise small pieces. You can always come back for more!

MAKES 25 SQUARES

TIME REQUIRED
20 minutes prep
25 minutes baking

BAKING CHALLENGE

Make this gluten-free

Replace the plain flour with gluten-free plain flour.

INGREDIENTS

200g (7oz) chocolate (white or milk)

150g (5oz) butter

275g (9¾oz) light brown sugar

½ teaspoon salt

2 eggs

1 teaspoon vanilla extract

200g (7oz) plain flour

20g (¾oz) cornflour

100g (3½oz) pecans, chopped (optional)

METHOD

1. Preheat the oven to 180°C fan (400°F/gas 6). Grease and line a 20cm (8") square tin.

2. Break the chocolate into big chunks. Lay half of these chunks over the base of the lined baking tin. Keep the other half for later.

3. Melt the butter in a large mixing bowl in the microwave. Add the sugar and salt and whisk together.

4. Crack in the eggs, add the vanilla and whisk until smooth.

5. Add in the plain flour and cornflour, and fold in with a spatula. Then add the pecans (if using) and remaining chocolate chunks from earlier. The batter should be smooth and shiny.

6. Pour this into the baking tin and bake for 25–30 minutes (it's perfect after 27 minutes in my oven) until the mixture has a good crust on top, the very edge feels and looks set, but the mixture wobbles a little when shaken from about 2cm (¾") in from the edge.

7. Cool at room temperature for about 30 minutes, then place in the fridge for at least 3 hours (preferably 5+ hours) to cool until cold (trust me, it's worth the wait). Slice into 25 squares.

Bake it your own

This cake will taste amazing frosted with the cream cheese frosting from the Carrot Patch Cupcake recipe on page 141.

Make this gluten-free

- ⭐ Replace the plain flour in the sponge with gluten-free plain flour.
- ⭐ Ensure the baking powder is gluten-free.

ANY REASON CHOCOLATE CAKE

This is an any-reason chocolate cake because you really can bake it for any reason. It's got enough wow factor to serve for a birthday or pudding at a dinner party. It's also quick and simple enough to throw together for a slice of mid-afternoon cake or just to bake for the joy of baking at any time.

The cake recipe is a go-to for me and is my favourite chocolate cake. The batter is very liquid (you will probably be surprised how liquid it is), but this makes the cake one of the softest and most moist you have ever had. The frosting is also a bit of a cheat. It takes 2 or 3 minutes to make but has great hazelnut and chocolate flavour from the chocolate spread.

TIME REQUIRED
15 minutes prep
25 minutes baking

BAKING CHALLENGE

INGREDIENTS

For the cake

85g (3oz) plain flour

40g (1½oz) cocoa powder

½ teaspoon baking powder

½ teaspoon bicarbonate of soda

130g (4½oz) light brown sugar

½ teaspoon salt

1 teaspoon vanilla extract

1 egg

90ml (¼ cup + 2 tablespoons) milk

50ml (3 tablespoons + 1 teaspoon) oil

60ml (¼ cup) boiling water

For the frosting

100ml (⅓ cup + 1 tablespoon) double cream

100g (3½oz) chocolate hazelnut spread

For decoration

20g (¾oz) hazelnuts, roasted

METHOD

BAKE THE CAKE

1. Preheat the oven to 170°C fan (375°F/gas 5). Grease and base line an 18cm (7") round cake tin with baking paper.
2. Sieve the flour, cocoa powder, baking powder and bicarbonate of soda into a bowl.
3. Add in the sugar and salt. Whisk in the vanilla, egg, milk and oil until smooth.
4. Measure the boiling water and slowly pour it into the mixture, whisking constantly.
5. Pour the thin batter into the prepared tin. Bake for 25–30 minutes or until a skewer comes out with only a few moist crumbs. Turn out to cool on a wire rack.

MAKE THE FROSTING

1. Whip the cream with the hazelnut spread using an electric mixer until it holds a trail from the whisk.
2. Spread over the top of the cooled sponge and sprinkle over chopped hazelnuts.

PLUM CRUMBLE TRAYBAKE

GFO

Crumble meets cake. This traybake layers soft, stewed fruit over a gently spiced cinnamon sponge, all topped with crunchy crumble. You can change the type of fruit you use for the filling to use a favourite of your own or to use up any leftovers sitting in the fruit bowl at home (see Crumble recipe on page 150 for a list of fruits you could use). The cake tastes fantastic warm with lashings of custard or cold on its own.

MAKES 16 SQUARES

TIME REQUIRED
35 minutes prep
25 minutes baking

BAKING CHALLENGE

INGREDIENTS

For the filling

300g (10½oz) plums, pitted and chopped

75g (2½oz) light brown sugar

15g (½oz) cornflour, plus 1 tablespoon water

For the sponge

120g (4¼oz) butter, softened

100g (3½oz) light brown sugar

100g (3½oz) self-raising flour

2 eggs

60g (2oz) ground almonds

½ teaspoon ground cinnamon

½ teaspoon baking powder

½ teaspoon salt

For the crumble topping

80g (2¾oz) plain flour

30g (1oz) porridge oats

½ teaspoon ground cinnamon

½ teaspoon salt

20g (¾oz) light brown sugar

60g (2oz) butter, melted

Make this gluten-free

- ☆ Replace the self-raising flour in the sponge with gluten-free self-raising flour.

- ☆ Ensure the baking powder in the sponge is gluten-free.

- ☆ Replace the plain flour in the crumble with gluten-free plain flour.

- ☆ Replace the oats in the crumble with gluten-free oats.

METHOD

1. Preheat the oven to 160°C fan (350°F/ gas 4). Grease and base line a 20cm (8") square cake tin.

MAKE THE FILLING

1. Heat the chopped plums and sugar over high heat until the plums start to release their juices.
2. Stir the cornflour with the water to create a slurry. Add this to the pan with the plums and cook over high heat whilst stirring until the mixture has thickened. Set aside to cool.

MAKE THE SPONGE

1. Cream the butter and sugar until light and fluffy. Add in all the remaining ingredients and mix until combined into a batter.

MAKE THE CRUMBLE TOPPING

1. Add all the ingredients, except the butter, into a bowl and combine. Pour over the melted butter and stir in with a fork, encouraging it to form clumps.

ASSEMBLE AND BAKE

1. Spread the sponge batter over the base of the lined cake tin. Top with the cooled plum filling in an even layer (it will mix in a little with the cake batter).
2. Sprinkle the clumpy crumble topping over the plum filling and bake for 25–30 minutes until a skewer inserted into the centre comes out without cake batter on it (it will be covered with some fruit).

Bake it your own

Instead of cooking off fruit and adding this onto the sponge, you can spread over about 150g (5oz) of jam. The layer of fruit won't be as thick, but it will still taste delicious.

CARROT PATCH CUPCAKES

GFO

Putting veg in a cake does sound like a weird idea, but carrot cake is a classic for a reason. The carrots make this an incredibly moist and soft cake. There is a little warm spice in the sponge and a crunch from the walnuts (but you can leave these out if you don't like them). Cream cheese frosting is sweet and creamy with a bit of zip and zing, and is also the perfect partner for these cupcakes.

I think the decoration is super cute, but if you're a little short on time, a batch of standard 'patchless' carrot cupcakes will still go down a treat with all your friends.

MAKES 10–12 CUPCAKES

TIME REQUIRED
20 minutes prep
15 minutes baking
30 minutes decorating

BAKING CHALLENGE

INGREDIENTS

For the cake

100g (3½oz) light brown sugar

100ml (½ cup) oil

2 eggs

140g (5oz) carrots, peeled (about 2–3 carrots)

100g (3½oz) walnuts, chopped

1 teaspoon vanilla extract

100g (3½oz) self-raising flour

1 teaspoon bicarbonate of soda

1 teaspoon ground cinnamon

½ teaspoon ground mixed spice

½ teaspoon salt

For the frosting

125g (4½oz) butter, softened

175g (6oz) icing sugar

175g (6oz) cream cheese

For decoration

75g (2½oz) chocolate biscuits (e.g. bourbons or oreos)

Orange gel food colour

Mint leaves

METHOD

MAKE THE CAKES

1. Preheat the oven to 170°C fan (375°F/gas 5). Fill a 12-hole muffin tin with brown cupcake cases.

2. Whisk together the sugar, oil and eggs in a large mixing bowl.

3. Grate the carrots using the big holes of a grater and weigh 140g (5oz) into the mixture. Add the walnuts and vanilla.

4. Sift over the flour, bicarbonate of soda, cinnamon and mixed spice. Add the salt and fold this all through until combined.

5. Fill the muffin cases about two-thirds full. Bake for about 15 minutes until a skewer inserted into the centre comes away clean. Leave to cool.

MAKE THE FROSTING

1. Beat the butter until smooth and light with an electric mixer. Add the icing sugar in three batches, beating for 2 minutes after each addition.

2. Add the cream cheese in three portions, mixing through until just combined after each addition. Fill a piping bag with the frosting.

DECORATE

1. Pipe a ring of frosting around the edge of each cupcake. You should have at least ¼ of the frosting remaining after.

2. Crush up the chocolate biscuits into a crumb by bashing them in a sealed bag with a rolling pin or in a food processor. Dip the frosting ring of each cupcake into the biscuit crumb, so it looks like soil.

3. Pipe out the remaining frosting into a bowl and mix through some orange food colour until it looks like a carrot colour. Fill a new piping bag, fitted with a large round nozzle (or cut a large hole from the bag), with the orange icing.

4. Pipe a tall blob of orange frosting onto the centre of each cupcake to resemble a carrot.

5. Top every carrot with some small mint leaves to look like carrot tops.

CHAPTER 7

PUDDING

SECRET SAUCE CHOCOLATE PUDDING

GFO

This pudding is magic! When you serve a piece to people at the table, they will be amazed when they see a silky-smooth sauce hiding underneath what looks like just a regular sponge and will want to know the secret. I'm giving you the secret of how this works in this recipe, but you can choose whether you let them know or not!

TIME REQUIRED

15 minutes prep
25 minutes baking

BAKING CHALLENGE

INGREDIENTS

For the sponge

100g (3½oz) butter

75g (2½oz) caster sugar

75g (2½oz) light brown sugar

½ teaspoon salt

150ml (½ cup + 2 tablespoons) milk

3 eggs

200g (7oz) self-raising flour

50g (1¾oz) cocoa powder

For the sauce

200g (7oz) light brown sugar

20g (¾oz) cocoa powder

250ml (1 cup + 1 tablespoon) boiling water

METHOD

1. Preheat the oven to 160°C fan (350°F/ gas 4).

2. Melt the butter in a pan or in the microwave. Pour this into a mixing bowl with the caster sugar, light brown sugar and salt and whisk to combine.

3. Add in the milk and eggs and whisk until combined.

4. Sift over the flour and cocoa powder and use a spatula to mix until combined into a batter. Pour this batter into an oven dish approx. 20cm x 30cm (8" x 12") and spread out to the edges.

5. Now make the sauce. Add the light brown sugar and cocoa powder for the sauce into a bowl. Pour in 250ml (1 cup) of boiling water and whisk until combined.

6. Pour this sauce directly over the top of the sponge mixture, and don't stir. This looks really weird, but it is correct!

7. Place the mixture with its watery top into the oven and bake for about 25–30 minutes until the cake top feels firm to the touch all over (bake it for less time if your dish is bigger, and you might need to bake it for longer if the dish is smaller).

8. The watery mixture will sink underneath the sponge during the baking to create a sauce at the bottom of the dish with the sponge floating on top. Serve warm with ice cream or cream.

Bake it your own

Chop up some nuts, chocolate chunks or marshmallows and mix into the sponge batter.

Make this gluten-free

Replace the self-raising flour with gluten-free self-raising flour.

CRUMBLE

Crumble is the ultimate comfort pudding. It's the perfect pudding for a cold winter night. I remember I used to pick the crumble topping away from the fruit because I didn't like the texture of cooked fruit. Now I love the fruit layer, but I still love the crumble topping as much as before.

It's worth trying lots of different fruits to find ones you like. The first cooked fruit I remember loving were berries. From there, I started to enjoy other cooked fruits more and more. Now I can't get enough stewed fruit. I've left the recipe just saying fruit, so you can pick your favourite, but I'll give you a list of fruits that will work fantastically in a crumble:

- ☆ Berries (fresh or frozen)
- ☆ Apples (peeled and cored)
- ☆ Pears (peeled and cored, or tinned)
- ☆ Peaches (pitted)
- ☆ Plums (pitted)
- ☆ Nectarines (pitted)
- ☆ Rhubarb

TIME REQUIRED

20 minutes prep
40 minutes baking

BAKING CHALLENGE

Make this gluten-free

- ☆ Replace the plain flour in the crumble with gluten-free plain flour.
- ☆ Replace the porridge oats with gluten-free porridge oats.

INGREDIENTS

For the fruit

1kg (2lb 3oz) fruit (see suggested
    fruits on the previous page)

100g (3½oz) sugar

15g (½oz) cornflour, plus
    2 tablespoons water

For the crumble

200g (7oz) plain flour

75g (2½oz) porridge oats

1 teaspoon salt

50g (1¾oz) light brown sugar

75g (2½oz) nuts, chopped (optional)

150g (5oz) butter, melted

METHOD

1. Preheat the oven to 170°C fan (375°F/gas 5).

MAKE THE FILLING

1. Wash and chop the fruit into approx. 2cm (¾")
   cubes. If the fruit has a tough skin (e.g. apples and
   pears), peel this before chopping and core or pit
   any fruits with a stone or tough core (e.g. plums and
   nectarines).

2. Add the fruit into a pan with the sugar over high heat
   for about 5 minutes until it releases some juices into
   the pan.

3. Mix the cornflour with water to create a slurry,
   add to the fruit and boil whilst stirring for a couple
   of minutes until the liquid around the fruit has
   thickened. Pour this into a deep oven dish.

MAKE THE CRUMBLE

1. Add all the ingredients, except the butter, into a
   bowl and combine. Pour over the melted butter and
   stir in with a fork, encouraging it to form clumps.

2. Sprinkle the clumps of crumble mixture in an even
   layer over the stewed fruit.

3. Bake in the oven for about 40 minutes until the
   crumble topping is a deep golden brown.

CROISSANT PUDDING

GFO

This is a delicious and indulgent version of a bread and butter pudding, a slightly odd-sounding dish of bread baked in custard. It sounds a little strange, but it is actually very tasty. This version uses croissants instead of bread, which makes a very rich pudding because of all the butter in the croissants. It's not the sort of pudding you could eat every day, but it's great for a treat every once in a while. I have added some raisins in with the pudding mainly because my friend who tested this pudding loves raisins. You could switch the raisins out for chocolate chips if you prefer.

TIME REQUIRED

25 minutes prep
20 minutes soaking
25 minutes baking

BAKING CHALLENGE

INGREDIENTS

300g (10½oz) croissants

50g (1¾oz) raisins

4 egg yolks + 1 egg

75g (2½oz) light brown sugar

1 large orange, zested and juiced

2 teaspoons cinnamon

½ teaspoon salt

300ml (1¼ cup) milk

200ml (¾ cup + 2 tablespoons)
   double cream

Bake it your own

You can use this recipe to make a traditional bread and butter pudding by substituting the croissant for regular bread. Spread a thin layer of butter over each slice of bread and cut into triangles before layering into your dish, covering with custard and baking.

Make this gluten-free

Replace the croissants with gluten-free croissants or brioche bread.

METHOD

1. Preheat the oven to 170°C fan (375°F/ gas 5). Gather an oven-safe dish with a capacity of approx. 1½ litres (1½ quart).

2. Slice the croissants in half and tightly pack them into the dish. Scatter the raisins over and between the croissant slices.

3. In a large bowl, whisk the eggs with the sugar, orange juice, cinnamon and salt until combined. Meanwhile, place the milk, cream and orange zest over high heat until it just begins to bubble (stirring every so often).

4. Slowly pour the hot milk mixture over the egg mixture, whisking all the time. You may need a set of big hands to help you with this step. This is a custard.

5. Pour the custard over the croissants in the dish. Leave to soak for 20–30 minutes.

6. Bake in the oven for 25–30 minutes. Serve hot.

BANOFFEE TARTE TATIN

 GFO

Tarte Tatin is a classic French dessert with caramelised soft apples sitting on crispy puff pastry. This version combines this traditional French dessert with the flavours of a banoffee pie. The bananas are nearly velvety and get a deep caramelly chew around the edges.

Serve it warm with a big scoop of ice cream melting over the top, and you're in for a treat!

TIME REQUIRED
20 minutes prep
30 minutes baking

BAKING CHALLENGE

INGREDIENTS

50g (1¾oz) light brown sugar

15g (½oz) butter

2 tablespoons double cream

3 large bananas

30g (1oz) walnuts, chopped (optional)

200g (7oz) puff-pastry (shop-bought)

METHOD

1. Preheat the oven to 190°C fan (410°F/gas 6). Grease and base line an 18cm (7") cake tin with baking paper.

2. Add the sugar, butter and cream into a pan. Stir over medium heat until the butter has melted and the mixture is smooth. This is your caramel layer. Pour over the base of the tin.

3. Slice the bananas into coins about 1.5cm (½") thick. Lay the coins over the caramel in the tin in a single layer. Fill any gaps between the bananas with chopped walnuts. Pile the remaining banana into the tin.

4. Roll out the puff pastry on a lightly floured surface into a rough circle shape about 20cm (8") across.

5. Drape the pastry over the top of the tin. Press the edges of the pastry down the side of the tin around the bananas using a table knife.

6. Cut a cross in the top of the pastry and bake in the oven for 30–35 minutes, or until the pastry is deep golden.

7. While the tarte is still hot, and with oven gloves on, place a serving plate over the top of the tin and flip the tin upside down to remove the tarte tatin (ask

Bake it your own

Replace the bananas with one of your favourite fruits, e.g. slice up apples, plums, pears, nectarines, apricots or even figs.

Make this gluten-free

Use gluten-free shop-bought pastry.

a grown-up for help if it's too tricky). Sometimes the bananas and baking paper get stuck at the bottom of the tin. This is okay, just pick out the bananas with a spoon and arrange back on the pastry base, and no one will even know this happened.

8. Serve warm – try it with cold ice cream or warm custard.

RASPBERRY, OAT & HONEY CHEESECAKE

This cheesecake is firmly inspired by my home, Scotland. Raspberries, oats and honey are some of the best ingredients grown and produced here and together make up one of my favourite flavour combos for a pudding.

I love the base on this cheesecake, so I have made it quite thick. The granola provides a lot of texture and crunch underneath the soft, smooth cream cheese filling. This whole pudding is very quick to put together, and you don't even need to turn the oven on.

GFO

TIME REQUIRED

30 minutes prep

BAKING CHALLENGE

INGREDIENTS

For the base
150g (5¼oz) oatcakes
150g (5¼oz) granola
125g (4½oz) butter, melted

For the filling
300ml (1¼ cups) double cream
75g (2½oz) icing sugar
500g (1lb 2oz) cream cheese
75g (2½oz) honey
250g (9oz) raspberries

For the topping
50g (1¾oz) granola
50g (1¾oz) raspberries

METHOD

1. Place the oatcakes in a food bag and bash them with a rolling pin until they are a fine crumb (alternatively, you can blitz them in a food processor).

2. Add the granola to the oatcake crumb and pour over the melted butter. Stir until evenly coated in butter.

3. Firmly press the oatcake mix into a flat layer over the base of a 20cm (8") loose-based tin with the base of a smaller cake tin or the back of a spoon. Place this in the fridge whilst you make the filling.

4. Whip the cream with the icing sugar until it holds its shape in medium peaks.

5. Briefly whisk the cream cheese and honey in a separate bowl until combined and smooth.

6. Fold the whipped cream into the cream cheese mixture until combined. Lightly crush the raspberries before stirring through the mixture until dispersed.

7. Pour the filling over the base and level off with the back of a spoon. Leave this in the fridge for at least 4 hours until set.

Bake it your own

☆ Use a different berry in place of raspberries.

☆ You can use a chocolate biscuit base for this cheesecake. Use the recipe for the base from the Chocolate Mousse Pie on page 99.

Make this gluten-free

☆ Replace the oatcakes in the base with gluten-free oatcakes or gluten-free digestive biscuits.

☆ Replace the granola in the base and for decoration with gluten-free granola.

8. Blow some hot air from a hairdryer around the outside of the tin to gently melt the edge of the cheesecake and make it easier to slide out. Stand the tin on a tall jar or mug and gently press down on the side of the tin to release the cheesecake.

9. Top the cheesecake with some granola and extra raspberries for decoration.

MANGO AND COCONUT PANNA COTTA

Panna cotta is a smooth, cold, set dessert from Italy. It is so quick and simple to make but tastes so dreamy and creamy. It's amazing. Panna cotta is also the perfect thing to prep for a dinner party or an evening that you want to cook for the family because it can be prepared ahead of time and is ready to serve straight from the fridge when you need it.

I have changed it from the classic a little by including some coconut milk and topping it with a mango puree. The mango puree comes straight from a tin of mango pulp, an amazing ingredient you can pick up in lots of big supermarkets. The flavour of this mango pulp is awesome. It requires zero prep and is not very expensive. The mango is bright and fresh, perfect to pair with the creamy panna cotta.

MAKES 4–6 PANNA COTTAS

TIME REQUIRED
10 minutes prep
2+ hours chilling

BAKING CHALLENGE

Bake it your own

☆ You can make a regular vanilla panna cotta by replacing coconut milk with whole milk.

INGREDIENTS

For the panna cotta

2 sheets leaf gelatine

200ml (¾ cup + 2 tablespoons) coconut milk alternative

40g (1½oz) caster sugar

1½ teaspoons vanilla extract

200ml (¾ cup + 2 tablespoons) double cream

For topping

200g (7oz) mango pulp (available in tins in the supermarkets)

20g (¾oz) toasted coconut flakes (optional)

METHOD

1. Cover the gelatine sheets in cold water for about 5 minutes until they have softened.

2. While the gelatine is softening, warm the coconut milk alternative in a saucepan with the sugar and vanilla until the sugar has dissolved, and the milk begins to steam.

3. Take the milk off the heat. Pick up the softened gelatine sheets with your hands, squeeze out the excess liquid and drop the sheets into the warm milk. Stir until the sheets have melted into the milk mixture.

4. Slowly pour the double cream into the warm milk whilst stirring.

5. Pour this mixture into 4–6 small glasses or cups and leave in the fridge to set for at least 2 hours.

6. Once the top of the panna cottas feel firm, gently spoon on a layer of mango pulp and then top with coconut flakes if you want.

NO-CHURN ICE CREAM

I am crazy about ice cream! I can't help but smile every time I eat it. The only issue with ice cream is that you really need a fancy ice cream machine to make it at home – except with this recipe! All you need is a bowl, an electric whisk and a tub to store the ice cream in the freezer. The fat content from the double cream and the form of sugar in the condensed milk means it will freeze smooth and soft without churning in a fancy machine. However, this ice cream is creamier than most, so you might only need small servings.

Ice cream should be fun, so go crazy with adding mix-ins into the mixture before freezing. Some ideas for good mix-ins are:

☆ Your favourite chocolate bars

☆ Biscuits and cookies

☆ Cookie dough (page 97, Cookie Dough Truffles)

☆ Granola

☆ Caramel sauce (page 131, STP Muffins)

☆ Chocolate Sauce

☆ Jam

☆ Curd

MAKES ABOUT 1 LITRE (1 QUART) OF ICE CREAM

TIME REQUIRED

10 minutes prep
4+ hours freezing

BAKING CHALLENGE

Bake it your own

You can still add any mix-ins you like to shop-bought ice cream. Allow it to soften for about 10 minutes out of the freezer, then stir in mix-ins of your choosing before refreezing.

INGREDIENTS

600ml (2⅓ cups) double cream

1 tin condensed milk (397g/14oz)

1 tablespoon vanilla bean paste

200–300g (7–11oz) mix-ins (sauces and chunks)

METHOD

1. Add the double cream, condensed milk and vanilla into a mixing bowl. Whisk with an electric mixer until it thickens and holds its shape in soft peaks.

2. Fold through your mix-ins (chop solid mix-ins into bitesize chunks). If folding through a sauce, don't mix it too much, so you are left with ripples through the ice cream.

3. Pour the ice cream into an ice cream tub or loaf tin, cover the surface with baking paper and freeze for at least 4 hours.

CHAPTER 8

AFTERNOON TEA

AFTERNOON TEA SANDWICHES

Afternoon tea always starts with sandwiches. It's tradition. This isn't so much a recipe but a couple of ideas for nice sandwich fillings you can put together to start a great afternoon tea!

THE BREAD

FOR CLOSED SANDWICHES

✶ Simple crusty loaf (in tin), page 49.

✶ Gluten-free loaf, page 51.

✶ Or just use shop-bought, ready sliced bread.

1. Slice the loaves into slices about ¾cm (¼"–½") thick. You always make thicker slices when you slice homemade bread, but the bread is so good that it doesn't matter!

2. To make super neat finger sandwiches, build a standard sandwich. Cut the crusts off the sandwich, making it a neat rectangle.

3. Cut the sandwich in two, lengthways, to create neat finger sandwiches ready for a fancy afternoon tea.

FOR OPEN SANDWICHES

✶ Dark soda bread, page 61.

✶ Or use a shop-bought loaf of bakery bread, unsliced.

1. Slice the bread into 1cm (½") thick, short slices. If using the soda bread from page 61 cut this into its 4 quarters and slice these into 1cm (½") slices.

2. Top the soda bread with the filling, piling it quite high.

THE FILLINGS

SPANISH HAM

Olive oil

Iberian ham (or prosciutto/another
    cured pork)

Watercress (or rocket)

1. Drizzle about 1 teaspoon olive oil onto each slice
of bread. Top with a couple of slices of ham and a
handful of rocket before closing the sandwich.

SMOKED SALMON AND CAPERS

Cream cheese

Capers, drained

Smoked salmon

1. Spread a thin layer of cream cheese over both sides
of bread. Top with some capers, then a layer of
smoked salmon before closing the sandwich.

HUMMUS AND SUNDRIED TOMATOES

Hummus

Sundried tomatoes (or jarred roasted
    peppers)

Gem lettuce leaves

1. Spread a layer of hummus onto each side of bread.
Top with a layer of sundried tomatoes and a layer of
gem lettuce leaves before closing the sandwich.

AVOCADO SANDWICH

1 avocado

Pinch salt

Handful coriander, chopped

½ lime, juice

½ red onion, finely diced (optional)

Cherry tomatoes, halved

1. Run a knife around the middle of the avocado along
the tall sides around the pit. Use your hands to split
the avocado in two to reveal the pit.

2. Use a spoon to dig out the pit. Then use a spoon to
scrape the avocado flesh out from the skin.

3. Finely chop the avocado on a board, then add it to a
bowl with a pinch of salt, coriander and the juice of
half a lime.

4. Mash it with a fork into a rough paste, then add in
the diced onion, if using. Taste the avocado and add
more seasoning until you like the taste.

5. Spread a thick layer of avocado over the bread, and
press the halved cherry tomatoes into the avocado
before closing the sandwich.

PESTO PALMIERS

GFO

It's quite nice to have one or two more savoury items alongside the sandwiches in an afternoon tea. These lovely little savoury swirls bring a delicious crunch to the starting dishes of an afternoon tea, perfect to serve alongside your sandwiches. These would also be amazing on the side of soup for lunch.

Palmiers are a French pastry shaped to look like a palm leaf or elephant ear. They are normally sweet, with sugar rolled into the puff pastry, but I've opted to put a savoury twist on them for this afternoon tea.

MAKES 20–30 PALMIERS

TIME REQUIRED

10 minutes prep
20 minutes chilling
20 minutes baking

BAKING CHALLENGE

INGREDIENTS

150g (5oz) puff pastry (shop-bought)

3 tablespoons pesto

METHOD

1. Preheat the oven to 190°C fan (410°F/gas 6). Line a baking tray with baking paper.
2. Roll out the pastry into a rectangle about 20cm x 30cm (8" x 12") on a lightly floured surface.
3. Top the pastry with the pesto and spread it evenly over it.
4. Tightly roll the pastry into a spiral from one of the long edges until you reach halfway.
5. Repeat on the other side of the pastry until the two rolls meet in the middle. Chill in the fridge for at least 20 minutes.
6. Cut slices about ¾cm (¼"–½") thick from the roll. They will squish a little as you slice them. Place these on the baking tray and reshape them on the tray with your hands.
7. Bake for about 20 minutes or until deeply golden. The outside palmiers often bake a lot faster than the inside ones, so you can switch them around about 15 minutes through the baking to encourage even browning.
8. Cool on the baking tray before digging in!

Bake it your own

You can make sweet palmiers with the same method. Instead of the pesto, when the pastry is rolled out, sprinkle over 50g (1¾oz) of sugar with an optional teaspoon of cinnamon before rolling up. Cut and bake as instructed above.

Make this gluten-free

Replace the puff pastry with shop-bought gluten-free puff pastry.

BRANDY SNAP BASKETS

Brandy snaps are a very thin, snappy little caramel-flavoured biscuit. When they come out of the oven, they are very soft, and as they cool, they harden into the crunchiest biscuit you will ever have. As they are cooling and firming up, there is a window of time when they are firm and cool enough to handle but still flexible enough to bend without breaking. This is when you can mould the brandy snap and turn it into a basket.

MAKES 16 BASKETS

TIME REQUIRED
30 minutes prep
40 minutes baking (in batches)

BAKING CHALLENGE

INGREDIENTS

For the brandy snaps
40g (1½oz) butter

40g (1½oz) light brown sugar

40g (1½oz) golden syrup

½ teaspoon salt

40g (1½oz) plain flour

For the filling
150ml (½ cup + 2 tablespoons) double cream

15g (½oz) icing sugar

1 teaspoon vanilla bean paste/extract

150g (5oz) fresh berries

METHOD

1. Preheat the oven to 180°C fan (400°F/gas 6). Line two baking trays with non-stick baking paper. Lightly grease the underside of a mini muffin tray or four tiny glasses with a little oil on a piece of kitchen roll.

MAKE THE BRANDY SNAPS

1. Gently heat the butter, sugar, syrup and salt in a pan over low heat until the butter has melted and the sugar has dissolved.

2. Remove the pan from the heat, throw in the flour and stir until combined into a smooth batter.

3. Pour a teaspoon measure of batter onto a lined baking tray with 3 other teaspoons of batter with lots of space in between. Bake one tray of the mixture for 7–9 minutes. The snaps should be deep golden all over, very flat and spread out and look lacy.

4. Remove from the oven and cool on the tray for 2–3 minutes until just warm to the touch. At this stage, they should be mouldable without breaking. Lift the snaps off the tray with a palette knife, then using your hands, mould the brandy snaps around the outside of the greased mini muffin tin or other moulds. Let the snap sit on the mould for a minute

until completely cool and firm before sliding it off the mould.

5. You need to work fast with the mixture while it is not too hot to touch, but before it becomes too cold and brittle to work around the moulds without snapping. If it does become too brittle to work with, place the baking tray back in the oven for a minute to soften the biscuits again.

6. Repeat the process of baking and moulding until you have used all of the batter.

MAKE THE FILLING

1. Whisk the cream with the icing sugar and vanilla until it is thick and just holds its shape.

2. Use two small spoons to fill each basket with the cream. Chop the berries and top each basket with a generous portion of them.

Bake it your own

★ Make classic brandy snap rolls:

★ Lightly oil the handle of a wooden spoon. When the brandy snaps are at the correct working temperature and consistency, roll it around the spoon handle until the two ends meet, creating a hollow tube. Hold it on the spoon for a couple of seconds before sliding off.

★ You don't always have to shape brandy snaps. You can leave them to cool flat, giving you a crunchy tuile that is perfect for serving with ice cream or a soft pudding.

Make this gluten-free

Replace the plain flour in the biscuits with gluten-free plain flour.

Baking Tip

If you want to make super neat scones, roll the dough out on a chopping board and let it rest in the fridge for 30 minutes before cutting. Rest again for an extra 20 minutes in the fridge before egg washing and baking.

SCONES

Scones are my favourite part of an afternoon tea, even though they are the simplest component. Given the option of a scone served with clotted cream and jam or a cake, I would choose the scone nine times out of ten. You can throw together a scone mix very fast and have hot scones out of the oven from start to finish in about 30 minutes. However, fancy hotels and places serving afternoon tea often have beautifully neat scones with straight sides. If you want to recreate these, you will need a bit more patience to wait for the dough to rest and relax. See the baking tip on the opposite page if you want to make professional-looking scones.

MAKES 8 SMALL SCONES

TIME REQUIRED
20 minutes prep
15 minutes baking

BAKING CHALLENGE

INGREDIENTS

For the scone dough
250g (9oz) self-raising flour
30g (1oz) caster sugar
1 teaspoon baking powder
½ teaspoon salt
35g (1¼oz) butter
1 egg
75ml (⅓ cup) milk

For the egg wash
1 egg yolk
Pinch of salt and sugar

Bake it your own

Add in 75g (2½oz) dried fruit or chocolate chips with the egg and milk whilst making the dough.

Make this gluten-free

☆ Replace the self-raising flour with gluten-free self-raising flour and ½ teaspoon xanthan gum.

☆ Ensure the baking powder is gluten-free.

METHOD

1. Preheat the oven to 190°C fan (410°F/ gas 6). Line two baking trays with baking paper.

2. Mix the flour, sugar, baking powder and salt in a bowl. Rub in the butter with your fingertips until no large clumps of butter remain.

3. Whisk the egg with the milk and add to the dry ingredients. Stir together with a table knife until beginning to form into a dough. Lightly knead the dough a couple of times until the mixture is fully combined.

4. Turn the dough out onto a well-floured surface. Roll out to a depth of just under 3cm (1"). Rub the edge of a round cutter approx. 5cm (2") in diameter with flour and cut straight down on the dough. Transfer the scones to the baking trays. Gently knead together the offcuts, re-roll and cut out more scones until you have used all the dough.

5. Mix the egg yolk with a pinch of salt and sugar to make an egg wash. Brush the tops of the scones with the egg wash before baking for 12–15 minutes.

STRAWBERRY & ELDERFLOWER CHOUX BUNS

GFO

Elderflower, lemon and strawberry are flavours that make me think of sunshine and summer days. This bake is a celebration of summer.

This is a choux pastry recipe which is one of the most challenging types of pastry to make. It is made by beating eggs into a paste made of water, milk, flour and butter. When you bake little mounds of this pastry, they release lots of steam inside, which makes them puff up and become hollow.

This is tricky, so it might take a couple of attempts to get it right, but stick with it. You will get better each time.

MAKES 8–12

TIME REQUIRED
45 minutes prep
20 minutes chilling
35 minutes baking

BAKING CHALLENGE

INGREDIENTS

For the craquelin (choux topping)

30g (1oz) butter, softened

30g (1oz) demerara sugar

30g (1oz) plain flour

For the choux

1 tablespoon + 2 teaspoons water

1 tablespoon + 2 teaspoons milk

20g (¾oz) butter

½ teaspoon caster sugar

¼ teaspoon salt

35g (1¼oz) strong bread flour

1 large egg, beaten

For the filling

150ml (½ cup + 2 tablespoons) double cream

10g (½oz) icing sugar

2 tablespoons elderflower cordial

1 lemon, zested

100g (3½oz) strawberry jam

To decorate

6 strawberries

METHOD

1. Preheat the oven to 175°C fan (375°F/ gas 5). Line two baking trays with baking paper.

MAKE THE CRAQUELIN TOPPING

1. Mix the butter, sugar and flour with a spoon until thoroughly combined.
2. Turn out the mixture onto a sheet of baking paper, cover with another sheet and use a rolling pin to roll out into as thin a sheet as you can. Place this sheet in the freezer until needed later.

MAKE THE CHOUX BUNS

1. Heat the water, milk, butter, sugar and salt in a pan until the butter has melted and the mixture begins to bubble.
2. Take it off the heat, immediately throw in the flour, and beat very fast to combine. Put the pan back on the heat, stir and press the thick mixture in the pan for 1–2 minutes.
3. Turn out the mixture into a mixing bowl and allow to cool for about 3 minutes. Once it is only slightly warm to the touch, add the beaten egg to the mixture in two steps, mixing with an electric hand mixer for a minute after each step.
4. Once you have added all the egg, the mixture should be thick and shiny. When lifted, it should fall off the whisk, leaving a 'V' shape behind.
5. Fill a piping bag with the mixture and cut a medium-sized hole in the bag. Pipe 8–12 circles measuring 2–3cm (¾"–1") onto the lined baking trays, leaving at least 2cm (¾") space between each bun.
6. Remove the craquelin from the freezer. Use a cookie cutter slightly larger than the choux buns to cut circles from the craquelin. Top each choux bun with a circle of craquelin.
7. Bake for about 30–35 minutes or until very deep brown, and they feel like they have a very firm crust. Check how brown they are after 20–25 minutes. If they are getting too dark, turn the oven temperature down to 165°C fan (350°F) for the remainder of the baking time.

MAKE THE FILLING

1. Whisk the cream with the icing sugar, cordial and lemon zest until it holds its shape.

2. Slice the top off every choux bun to reveal the hollow interior. You may need to cut away at the inside of the bun to create a hollow centre.

3. Spoon a little jam into the bottom of each bun. Spoon or pipe in the cream to fill the bun. Top with the choux bun lids.

4. Halve the strawberries and stick one strawberry half on the buns, sticking them down with a little extra cream.

Make this gluten-free

☆ Replace the plain flour in the craquelin with gluten-free plain flour.

☆ Replace the strong bread flour in the choux pastry with gluten-free self-raising flour and ¼ teaspoon xanthan gum.

Bake it your own

Use your favourite berry and jam in place of strawberries. I think blackberries would be particularly excellent.

ORANGE DRIZZLE CAKE

Everyone knows lemon drizzle cake, but using lemon's citrus cousin is less common. The orange drizzle is sweeter and less sharp than lemons, making the cake feel gentler. I have added ground almonds into the sponge. The flavour of almond pairs wonderfully with orange. In addition, ground almonds are fantastic for keeping a sponge moist and soft for longer once baked.

MAKES 25 SQUARES

TIME REQUIRED

15 minutes prep
25 minutes baking

BAKING CHALLENGE

Bake it your own

Orange works very well with rosemary. You can try adding 1 teaspoon of very finely chopped rosemary into the cake batter to get a pleasant fragrant taste from the rosemary in the sponge.

Make this gluten-free

- ☆ Replace the self-raising flour with gluten-free self-raising flour.
- ☆ Ensure the baking powder is gluten-free.

INGREDIENTS

For the cake

175g (6oz) unsalted butter, softened

175g (6oz) caster sugar

½ teaspoon salt

2 large oranges, zest

150g (5oz) self-raising flour

50g (1¾oz) ground almonds

½ teaspoon baking powder

3 eggs

1 teaspoon orange extract (optional)

For the topping

100g (3½oz) granulated sugar

½ large orange, juice

Orange zest

METHOD

1. Preheat the oven to 160°C fan (350°F/ gas 4). Grease and base line a 20cm (8") square tin with baking paper.

2. Cream the butter, sugar, salt and orange zest until light and fluffy. Add all the remaining cake ingredients into the bowl and mix until combined into a batter.

3. Add the batter into the tin, level off and bake for about 25–30 minutes. A skewer inserted into the centre of the cake should come out clean, and it should feel firm to the touch.

4. When the cake is just out of the oven, mix the granulated sugar and orange juice into a grainy mix.

5. Spoon the grainy syrup over the cake whilst still in the tin, spreading the sugar evenly over the cake. Allow it to cool completely in the tin. The syrup will soak into the sponge, and the sugar will form a crust on the outside of the cake.

6. Cut into squares and zest over some extra orange zest before serving.

LITTLE PAVLOVAS

GF

I think every part of an afternoon tea should be quite small and dainty. One of the joys of eating an afternoon tea is that you get to try lots of different bakes because they are all little versions. These wee pavlovas take the classic dessert and miniaturise it so it can sit well with an afternoon tea.

Most pavlovas are filled with a whipped cream filling, but I have chosen to go with a filling made of Greek yoghurt and some honey. The yoghurt is fresher than cream and helps keep these pavlovas a light summery dessert, making it a great bake to finish off your afternoon tea, when you will probably be quite full of lots of baking.

MAKES ABOUT 10

TIME REQUIRED
20 minutes prep
40 minutes baking

BAKING CHALLENGE

INGREDIENTS

For the meringue

2 egg whites

120g (4½oz) caster sugar

1 teaspoon cornflour

1 teaspoon lemon juice

For the filling

30g (1oz) honey

300g (10½oz) Greek-style yoghurt

2 peaches or nectarines

100g (3½oz) blackberries

30g (1oz) toasted flaked almonds (optional)

METHOD

MAKE THE MERINGUE

1. Preheat the oven to 110°C fan (265°F/gas 1). Line two baking trays with baking paper.

2. Add the egg whites to a large mixing bowl. Whisk with an electric hand whisk on full speed for about 1 minute until the egg whites are very frothy and thickening.

3. Mix the caster sugar and cornflour together. Add this 1 tablespoon at a time to the egg whites, whisking for 20 seconds at medium-high speed between each addition. This will take about 3–4 minutes.

4. The mixture should be very shiny and thick enough to hold its shape in stiff peaks. If you want a bit of fun, you can hold the bowl of meringue upside down. If made well, it should stay in the bowl (don't try this if your mixture looks runny after adding all the sugar; if it does, just start again!).

5. Add the lemon juice to the meringue and briefly whisk this in until combined.

Bake it your own

You can use this recipe to make a single larger pavlova. Spread out all the mixture onto a single baking tray and shape into a round of about 15cm–20cm (6"–8") in diameter. This will take longer to bake, about 1 hour.

6. Fill a piping bag with the meringue and pipe 10 portions of meringue onto baking trays about 6–7cm (2½"–3") in diameter. Alternatively, you can spoon portions of meringue onto the baking tray. Use a teaspoon to press into the centre of each meringue and run around to create a divot.

7. Bake the meringues in the oven for 35–45 minutes. They should feel firm to the touch and peel away from the paper if lifted off gently. Leave them in for another 10 minutes if they stick to the paper.

8. Remove from the oven when baked and leave to cool.

MAKE THE FILLING

1. Stir the honey into the yoghurt. You can use more or less than I have suggested, just give it a taste and make it as sweet as you like.

2. Slice the peaches or nectarines around their centre around the pit, and twist the two halves away from each other to separate. Scoop the stone out using a teaspoon. Cut the peach halves into a small dice, about 1cm (½").

3. Slice the blackberries in half.

4. Just before serving, fill the hole of the cooled pavlovas with the yoghurt. Top with the peaches and blackberries, followed by some flaked almonds and a drizzle of honey if you want.

CHAPTER 9
PARTY
BAKES

BIRTHDAY
THE PBP CAKE

A party in cake form! The Peter's Baking Party/Peanut Butter Piñata Cake. Four layers of chocolate sponge, all sandwiched with a salty-sweet peanut butter frosting and filled with a chocolate candy surprise!

With its vibrant colour and fun reveal, this cake will be a stand-out centrepiece at any party.

Note: I added extra sweets to this cake to enhance the pinata effect once it was cut. If you want to have an impressive pinata fall out, you need to cut a big first slice from the cake, and you can always add more sweets to it like me (you want all your friends to go wow!).

TIME REQUIRED
30 minutes prep
25 minutes baking
1 hour assembly

BAKING CHALLENGE

INGREDIENTS

For the cake
225g (8oz) butter, softened
225g (8oz) caster sugar
175g (6oz) self-raising flour
50g (1¾oz) cocoa powder
1½ teaspoons baking powder
4 eggs
½ teaspoon salt

For the peanut butter frosting
125g (4½oz) butter, softened
300g (10½oz) smooth peanut butter (use the creamy thick stuff, not natural)
225g (8oz) icing sugar
½ teaspoon salt
2–5 tablespoons milk

Decorations
150g (5oz) chocolate-covered peanut candies
100g (3½oz) rainbow sprinkles

METHOD

MAKE THE CAKE

1. Preheat the oven to 160°C fan (350°F/gas 4). Grease and base line 2 x 18cm (7") round cake tins.
2. Cream the butter and sugar until light and fluffy.
3. Sift over the flour, cocoa powder and baking powder. Add in the eggs and salt, and mix until just combined.
4. Split the mixture between the two tins, level off and bake for 25–30 minutes and a skewer inserted into the centre comes out clean. Leave to cool.

MAKE THE PEANUT BUTTER FROSTING

1. Beat the butter with an electric whisk until light and creamy.
2. Add in the peanut butter, icing sugar and salt, and beat for a couple of minutes. Whisk through the milk to create a smooth, soft, spreadable consistency that holds its shape. Add the milk one tablespoon at a time until you are happy with the texture.

ASSEMBLE AND DECORATE

1. Slice the two chocolate cakes in half widthways. You now have four thin cakes.

2. Set one of the bottom half slices aside. With the remaining three slices, cut a hole in the centre of each with a 6–7cm (2½") cookie cutter.

3. Secure one of the cut-out slices onto your serving plate with some frosting. Spread an even layer of frosting over the sponge and top with another layer. Repeat this until you have used the three layers with holes. Spread a layer of frosting over this top layer.

4. Fill the cavity of the cake with chocolate peanut candies.

5. Top the cake with the final layer of sponge, cut side down.

6. Spread a very thin layer of frosting around the outside of the cake with a palette knife and leave it in the fridge for at least 20 minutes to firm up.

7. Use the remaining frosting to cover the cake in a second layer.

8. Wash your hands before this next bit! Hold some sprinkles in your palm and press them onto the cake sides and top. Get a helping pair of hands to hold the cake over a large roasting tin as you do this, so the excess sprinkles are caught. You can reuse the caught sprinkles to cover the cake and fill in gaps.

Make this gluten-free

✭ Replace the self-raising flour in the sponge with gluten-free self-raising flour.

✭ Ensure the baking powder is gluten-free.

✭ Ensure you use gluten-free sweets to fill the cake.

Bake it your own

✭ Crumble up the discarded cake centres and press the crumbs onto the outside of the cake instead of sprinkles.

✭ Use your favourite chocolates to fill the centre of the cake.

✭ Go all out with any decoration you like!

EASTER
GIANT HOT CROSS BUN

There's something about making small things big and big things small that makes them all the more exciting! A hot cross bun is a nice thing to bake around Easter, but a giant hot cross bun is much cooler. It takes a standard Easter bake and turns it into a showstopping centrepiece for an Easter table. Another bonus about making one giant bun instead of multiple is that it's quicker and easier to shape. You can, of course, use this recipe to make smaller buns as well; it's just not quite as fun.

TIME REQUIRED

25 minutes prep
1 hour 30 minutes proving
45 minutes baking

BAKING CHALLENGE

INGREDIENTS

For the dough

410g (14oz) strong bread flour

60g (2oz) light brown sugar

1 teaspoon ground cinnamon

½ teaspoon mixed spice

1 teaspoon salt

2 teaspoons fast-action dried yeast

35g (1¼oz) butter

190ml (¾ cup + 1 tablespoon) milk

1 egg

100g (3½oz) raisins

50g (1¾oz) mixed peel

For the cross

50g (1¾oz) strong bread flour

50ml (3 tablespoons + 1 teaspoon) water

For the glaze

15g (½oz) honey

METHOD

MAKE THE DOUGH

1. Add the flour, sugar, cinnamon, mixed spice, salt and yeast to a bowl.

2. Gently warm the butter and milk in a pan until the butter has melted. Pour this into the bowl and stir with a table knife. Crack in the egg and stir again with a table knife until it comes together into a very shaggy dough with lots of dry patches.

3. Tip the dough onto a work surface and knead for 5–8 minutes until it is no longer sticking to the work surface and is quite a lot smoother than before.

4. Add half of the raisins and mixed peel onto the dough and knead through until combined. Repeat with the remaining raisins and mixed peel.

5. Place the dough back in the mixing bowl, cover with cling film or a tea towel and leave to prove for at least 30 minutes.

6. Remove the dough from the bowl and flatten it onto a lightly floured work surface. Pull the edges of the dough tightly together into the centre of the loaf.

7. Flip the loaf over onto the seam to show a smooth top. Press the sides of your hands into the base of

the dough whilst turning it slightly to encourage the loaf to be round.

8. Gently lift the dough onto a baking tray lined with baking paper and loosely cover with clingfilm brushed with a little oil or a tea towel.

9. Set aside in a warm place for 45 minutes–1 hour 30 minutes until nearly doubled in size and puffy.

10. Preheat the oven at this stage to 160°C fan (350°F/gas 4).

Bake it your own

- For a luxury hot cross bun, you can substitute the raisins and mixed peel for chocolate chips.

- To make individual buns, split the dough into 6 pieces before rolling each into buns and placing them on a baking paper-lined baking tray. Cover them with cling film to prove. Cut a smaller hole from the piping bag to pipe over crosses before baking for 20–25 minutes.

MAKE THE CROSS

1. Mix the 50g (1¾oz) of strong bread flour with 50ml (3 tablespoons + 1 teaspoon) of water and stir until combined into a thick paste. Fill a piping bag with this mixture.

2. Once the dough has proved, cut a medium-sized hole in the piping bag. Pipe a line across the middle of the loaf, then pipe another line in the other direction to make the cross.

3. Bake the loaf for 30 minutes until deep brown, then cover it with foil and bake for a further 15–20 minutes.

4. Once baked, allow it to cool completely then make the glaze. Gently warm the honey in the microwave for about 5 seconds and brush this all over the loaf to make it shiny.

CHRISTMAS
CHOCOLATE RUDOLPH

I'm not such a big fan of making complicated novelty cake designs; my goal is always to make them simple but effective. This cake demonstrates that well. A couple of easy-to-shape fondant and chocolate features, and you can create the cutest chocolate reindeer you ever could see.

This cake recipe is a simple vanilla sponge but loaded with chocolate chunks. These typically fall to the bottom of the sponges and go almost crunchy as it bakes. It's filled and covered with chocolate buttercream. Once again simple, but oh so tasty!

TIME REQUIRED

30 minutes prep
30 minutes baking
20 minutes decoration

BAKING CHALLENGE

INGREDIENTS

For the sponge

225g (8oz) butter, softened

225g (8oz) caster sugar

225g (8oz) self-raising flour

1½ teaspoons baking powder

4 eggs

½ teaspoon salt

200g (7oz) chocolate, chopped
  into chunks

For the chocolate buttercream

200g (7oz) butter, softened

½ teaspoon salt

320g (11oz) icing sugar

40g (1½oz) cocoa powder

3 tablespoons milk

For the decorations

100g (3½oz) dark chocolate

30g (1oz) red fondant

30g (1oz) white fondant

5g (¼oz) black fondant

Icing sugar, for dusting

Make this gluten-free

☆ Substitute the self-raising flour in the sponge for gluten-free self-raising flour.

☆ Ensure the baking powder in the sponge is gluten-free.

METHOD

MAKE THE CAKE

1. Preheat the oven to 160°C fan (350°F/ gas 4). Grease and base line 2 x 18cm (7") round cake tins.

2. Cream the butter and sugar with an electric whisk until light and fluffy.

3. Add the flour, baking powder, eggs and salt, and mix until combined. Stir the chopped chocolate into the batter to mix.

4. Split the mixture between the two tins, level off and bake for 30–35 minutes, or until a skewer inserted into the centre comes out clean. Leave to cool.

MAKE THE CHOCOLATE BUTTERCREAM

1. Beat the butter and salt with an electric whisk until very light and smooth.

2. Sift over half of the icing sugar and cocoa powder and beat for about 2 minutes. Start the whisk on low speed, then increase to high speed once the dry ingredients have been mixed in.

3. Sift over the remaining icing sugar and cocoa powder. Add in the milk and beat this for about 2 minutes until smooth.

4. It should be a soft, spreadable consistency that holds its shape. If it's too thick, add in some more milk a tablespoon at a time. If it's too thin, add in more icing sugar, 50g (1¾oz) at a time.

ASSEMBLE THE CAKE

1. Slice the two cooled cakes horizontally to create 4 layers of cake. If the cakes are very domed, you can trim the top off the cakes to make them flat. This will make a neater stacked cake.

2. Place one layer of cake on your serving plate. Spread over a thin layer of buttercream and top with the following sponge layer. Repeat this up the cake. Place the two bottom layers of sponge at the bottom of the cake and top with the two top layers of sponge.

3. Spread a thin layer of buttercream over the cake with a palette knife and set it in the fridge to chill for at least 20 minutes.

4. Take the cake out of the fridge and spread the remaining buttercream over the cake. I like to spread the buttercream over in many spreads to create a rougher texture that almost looks like fur.

MAKE THE CHOCOLATE ANTLERS

1. Draw two big antlers on a sheet of baking paper about 15cm (6") long with a pencil. Copy the picture on the next page. Flip the baking paper over, so the pencil is on the bottom. You should be able to see the outline of the pencil through the paper.

2. Melt the chocolate in the microwave or over a pan of simmering water and fill a piping bag with the chocolate.

3. Cut a hole from the piping bag and pipe around the outlines of the antlers as best as you can. Fill up the antlers

with the remaining chocolate and leave it at room temperature to set. You can also just spoon the chocolate over the template instead of piping, although it might not be as neat.

4. If the chocolate hasn't set after 30 minutes, place it in the fridge to chill and set, but don't put it in the fridge before the 30 minutes is up, or it won't set as well.

MAKE THE FONDANT NOSE AND EYES

1. Roll out the red fondant on a surface lightly dusted with icing sugar to about 1cm (½") thick. Use a 6cm (2½") cookie cutter to cut a circle of the fondant. Press the edges of the circle to make it into a rough oval shape.

2. Roll out the white fondant to about 1cm (½") thick. Cut two 2½cm (1") circles from it using a cookie cutter.

3. Roll tiny balls from the black fondant. Lightly wet the white fondant circles and press on the black fondant balls to create the eyes.

MAKE THE REINDEER COME TO LIFE

1. Stick the red nose and eyes onto the side of the cake to create the reindeer's face.

2. Use a knife to cut two slits into the top of the cake. Press the antlers into these slits.

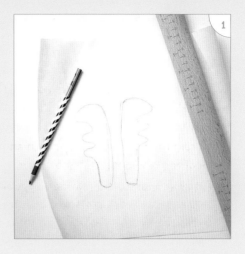

SPRING
LEMON MERINGUE TOWER

This is less baking, more assembling, but it's nice to have some simple ideas for easy-to-make desserts up your sleeve. Lemon feels like a natural spring flavour to me, and meringues are a great dessert around this time of year because they are a lot lighter and less rich than many cakes and puddings.

This looks very smart as a plated dessert. It's safest to stack these only 3 or 4 meringues tall, and that will look very good as a plated dessert. However, if you want to live on the edge, you can build it as high as you like! If stacking it tall, you should serve it quickly and be prepared for the chance of it toppling. If it does topple, you can always crush it up, serve it in bowls and call it Eton mess! If you stack them low and leave them in the fridge for a couple of hours, the meringues will soften, and they will all merge together into a soft cake-like consistency all the way through. If you like the meringues to stay crunchy, serve them straight away.

TIME REQUIRED
20 minutes

BAKING CHALLENGE

Bake it your own

☆ You can substitute the whipped cream for Greek yoghurt. This makes the dessert even lighter and fresher, perfect for warmer evenings. The slight tang from the yoghurt works well with the sweet meringue.

☆ Try adding fresh berries, chopped fruits or chopped nuts to the top of the meringue tower.

INGREDIENTS

150ml (½ cup + 2 tablespoons) double cream

15g (½oz) icing sugar

8–16 meringue nests

150g (5oz) lemon curd

To decorate (optional)

Edible flowers (can be bought dried from cake decorating companies, or fresh online)

METHOD

1. Whip the cream and icing sugar until soft and just holding its shape.

2. Stick a meringue nest onto a serving plate with a bit of cream. Spread a layer of lemon curd onto the meringue and top with a layer of whipped cream.

3. Top this with another meringue nest and repeat the filling process.

4. You can stack the meringues as high as you like, but the taller you go, the wobblier they become! Two or three meringues high is a good height for an individual or two-person dessert.

5. You can leave a low-stacked tower in the fridge for a couple of hours or overnight if you want it to soften or serve it straight away for crisp meringue.

6. Top the meringue cake with edible flowers, if you want, to give an even more spring-like feel.

SUMMER
BERRIES & CREAM CAKE

GFO

Britain grows some of the best berries in the world during the summer months. This cake is a celebration of the British summer. It wouldn't feel out of place at Wimbledon, where the classic dish served is simply strawberries and cream. It's the perfect thing to serve as the main event at a summer picnic or get together.

Berries feature heavily in lots of my baking. As well as tasting amazing, they also make any bake look immediately stunning with their almost jewel-like appearance.

The sponge I am using in this cake is called a Génoise. It is a very light and airy sponge from France made by whipping eggs for a long time, so they capture lots of bubbles and air. When folding in the flour, you have to be quite gentle with the sponge to make sure it doesn't deflate. The sponge will become quite dense if it's overmixed, so be gentle and as soon as you can't see any flour left in the batter, stop mixing.

TIME REQUIRED

20 minutes prep
20 minutes baking
20 minutes assembly

BAKING CHALLENGE

INGREDIENTS

For the Génoise sponge

65g (2¼oz) butter

5 eggs

150g (5oz) caster sugar

150g (5oz) self-raising flour

For the berries

500g (1lb 2oz) berries

40g (1½oz) caster sugar

For the cream

300ml (1¼ cup) double cream

30g (1oz) icing sugar

2 teaspoons vanilla bean paste or extract

For the soak

50ml (3 tablespoons + 1 teaspoon) milk

METHOD

MAKE THE SPONGE

1. Preheat the oven to 160°C fan (350°F/gas 4). Grease and base line 2 x 18cm (7") cake tins.

2. Melt the butter in a pan or the microwave. Pour into a separate container to allow it to cool. It should be liquid but barely warm when used.

3. Whisk the eggs and caster sugar together in a large bowl with an electric whisk for about 5 minutes. The mixture should be about three times its original volume, very thick and pale in colour.

4. Sieve over the flour and use a spatula to fold this into the mixture gently. Scrape around the edges and bottom of the bowl into the middle to mix all of the batter.

5. Once nearly all the flour is mixed in, pour the melted and cooled butter around the side of the bowl. Fold this in with the spatula until just combined. Stop mixing as soon as all the butter has been incorporated. Continuing to mix will deflate the batter and make a dense cake.

6. Split this mixture between the two tins and bake for 20–25 minutes, or until a skewer inserted into the centre comes out clean.

PREP THE BERRIES

1. Chop the berries to bitesize pieces. I leave raspberries and blueberries whole, cut blackberries in half and strawberries into four.

2. Place the berries in a bowl and sprinkle over the sugar. Stir to combine and set aside for about 15 minutes. The berries will release some juice in this time.

3. Pour the berry mix into a sieve over a bowl to separate the liquid and the berries. Keep both for later.

MAKE THE CREAM

1. Add the cream, icing sugar and vanilla into a large bowl. Whip with an electric whisk until it becomes thick and just holds onto the whisk when lifted from the bowl.

ASSEMBLE THE CAKE

1. Cut both the cooled cakes in half across to create four layers.

2. Pour the berry liquid that has dripped through the sieve into a new bowl. Add 50ml (3 tablespoons + 1 teaspoon) of milk to this and mix.

3. Place one layer of cake on your serving plate and use a pastry brush to brush some of the berry milk soak onto the sponge layer.

4. Cover the cake with a quarter of the cream and spread to the edges.

5. Spoon over a quarter of the berries and spread them out over the cream.

6. Top with another layer of sponge and repeat the soaking and filling up the cake, finishing the top of the cake with a layer of cream and pile of berries.

Make this gluten-free

Replace the self-raising flour in the sponge with gluten-free self-raising flour.

AUTUMN
PEAR CAKE

Things are starting to get darker and colder in autumn, running towards the winter months. At this time of year, it's nice to cook and bake things that are a bit warming and comforting as the nights draw in. This cake pairs pears with gentle cinnamon spice and light caramel flavour from the brown sugar sponge. Pears are in season during autumn, but I'm using tinned pears here, which means you could make this at any time of year.

TIME REQUIRED

20 minutes prep
25 minutes baking
30 minutes assembly

BAKING CHALLENGE

INGREDIENTS

For the cake

225g (8oz) butter, softened

225g (8oz) light brown sugar

225g (8oz) self-raising flour

1½ teaspoons baking powder

2 teaspoons cinnamon

4 eggs

½ teaspoon salt

For the filling and topping

1 tin (397g/14oz) pears

150g (5oz) mascarpone

300ml (1¼ cup) double cream

50g (1¾oz) light brown sugar

1 fresh pear, to decorate

METHOD

1. Preheat the oven to 160°C fan (350°F/gas 4). Grease and base line 2 x 18cm (7") round cake tins.

MAKE THE CAKE

1. Cream the butter and sugar until light and fluffy.
2. Add in the remaining cake ingredients and mix until just combined.
3. Split the mixture between the two tins, level off and bake for 25–30 minutes, until a skewer inserted into the centre comes out clean. Leave to cool.

MAKE THE FILLING

1. Drain the pears in a sieve over a bowl. Keep the juice or syrup for later.
2. Slice the pears into slices about ½cm (¼") thick.
3. Add the mascarpone, cream and brown sugar into a bowl and whisk with an electric whisk until it just holds its shape but is still soft. Fill a piping bag with the cream.

Make this gluten-free

- Replace the self-raising flour in the sponge with gluten-free self-raising flour.

- Ensure the baking powder in the sponge is gluten-free.

Bake it your own

- You can use fresh pear instead of tinned pears. Peel, core and slice two pears into ½cm (¼") slices. Then simmer them in a mixture of 75g (2½oz) light brown sugar and 250ml (1 cup) water for about 15 minutes until softened.

- You can fill the cake with a stewed fruit mixture. Double the quantities of the stewed fruit filling shown in the Plum Crumble Traybake recipe on page 139.

ASSEMBLE THE CAKE

1. Slice the cooled cakes in half across to create four layers of sponge.

2. Lay one layer of sponge onto your serving plate. Brush over some of the pear juice/syrup using a pastry brush.

3. Hold the piping bag vertically and pipe blobs of the cream over the sponge all around the perimeter. Pipe a little more cream into the centre of the cake and spread out into a fairly thin layer with the back of a spoon.

4. Lay pear slices over the cream in the centre of the sponge. Top this with another layer of sponge and repeat until you top the cake with the final layer of sponge.

5. Dust the sponge with icing sugar, pipe a final dod of cream on the centre and top with a small slice of fresh pear to decorate. If waiting to serve the cake for more than a couple of hours, rub the pear slice with a bit of lemon juice to prevent it from browning.

WINTER
GINGERBREAD HOUSE

This is a feat of both great baking and engineering. A gingerbread house doesn't only need to sit on a dinner table. During the winter and Christmas months, it can be used as decoration around the house. Once constructed, a gingerbread house can stay standing for a very long time, basically as long as you can stop yourself from digging into it.

I have given you the recipe for the gingerbread and icing and the templates to copy so you can construct your house, but how you go about decorating is entirely up to you. Get creative with the sweets you throw on there, or use other edible decorations like sprinkles, cereals, nuts, fondant decorations, etc. It takes quite a lot of care and attention to get the structure baked and built, but once you have a standing house, you can take as much time as you like to have fun and go wild with the decorations.

TIME REQUIRED

45 minutes prep
15 minutes baking
1 hour assembly and decoration.

BAKING CHALLENGE

Make this gluten-free

Replace the plain flour in the gingerbread with gluten-free plain flour and add 1 teaspoon of xanthan gum.

INGREDIENTS

For the gingerbread

175g (6oz) butter

125g (4½oz) dark muscovado sugar

100g (3½oz) golden syrup

450g (1lb) plain flour

1½ teaspoons bicarbonate of soda

½ teaspoon salt

1½ teaspoons ground ginger

1½ teaspoons ground cinnamon

½ teaspoon ground nutmeg

3 boiled sweets, optional

For the royal icing

40g (1½oz) pasteurised egg whites (1 egg white)

1 teaspoons lemon juice

240g (8½oz) icing sugar

METHOD

MAKE THE GINGERBREAD

1. Preheat the oven to 180°C fan (400°F/gas 6). Gather two baking trays. Copy the templates from the diagram onto a flattened cereal box and cut these out.

2. Add the butter, sugar and syrup into a pan over a low heat. Stir occasionally until the butter has melted and all the sugar has dissolved.

3. Meanwhile, add the flour, bicarbonate of soda, salt and spices into a large mixing bowl and stir to combine. Add in the liquid sugar and butter mixture and stir into the dry mix until most of the flour has been incorporated.

4. Allow to cool until barely warm to the touch, then tip out onto your work surface and knead for a couple of minutes until a bit smoother.

5. Roll out the dough between two big sheets of baking paper to about ¾cm (¼"–½") thick. Cut out as many template shapes from this portion of dough as possible. You need

2 x front/back, 2 x sides and 2 x roof. Cut the baking paper around each shape you have cut out and move these onto your baking trays on their baking paper.

6. Re-roll the offcuts between baking paper to ¾cm (¼"–½") and cut the remaining template shapes you need. With any remaining dough, you can roll it out and cut little biscuits of any shape. Christmas trees will look great and can stand next to the finished house.

7. From the front of the house, cut out a small door and two small windows with a 3cm (1") cookie cutter.

8. From the back of the house, cut out a small window with a 4cm (1½") cookie cutter.

9. From the sides of the house, cut out 2 small windows with a 3cm (1") cookie cutter.

My gingerbread house measures . . .

Roof x2
17cm (6½") long and 14cm (5½") wide.

Front & back
13cm (5") wide across the base, 8cm (3") up to the corner of the roof, 6½cm (2½") from the corner of the roof to the middle of the width and 10cm (4") from there to the point of the roof.

Side x2
12cm (4¾") width and 8cm (8") tall.

10. Keep the door intact to bake off. Re-roll the window cutouts and cut out more biscuits.

11. Crush the boiled sweets in a food bag with a rolling pin.

12. Bake the biscuits in the oven for about 7 minutes. Remove from the oven and sprinkle the crushed sweets into the windows of the house in a thin layer. Place the biscuits back in the oven for 3–4 more minutes until the sweets have melted and the biscuits are firm around the edges.

13. Leave the biscuits to cool on the baking trays.

MAKE THE ROYAL ICING

1. Whisk the egg whites until frothy. Add the lemon juice and whisk in the icing sugar in four batches with an electric hand mixer. When adding the icing sugar, start slow, then increase the speed once most of the icing sugar is incorporated.

2. The mixture should be firm, thick and able to hold its shape. Fill a piping bag fitted with a small round nozzle with the royal icing.

ASSEMBLE THE HOUSE

NOTE: This can be difficult to do by yourself. You might want to grab a helper to help hold all the pieces together while building the house.

1. Pipe a border of royal icing around the door frame and windows of the house.

2. Pipe royal icing onto the bottom edge of the house front and press this down on the serving board. Pipe down one of the inside edges and press a house side with royal icing piped onto its bottom edge into this to join. Repeat this with the other side of the house, pipe down the open edges of the sides, and attach the back of the house. Leave this to set for about 15 minutes.

3. Pipe royal icing down the slanted sides of the front and back of the houses and attach the roof pieces to these. The roof should slightly overhang the front, back and sides of the house. Hold the roof in place for about 3–5 minutes until it has set enough not to slide off.

4. Pipe royal icing along all of the open edges of the roof to look like snow. Use a toothpick to ruffle these royal icing borders and give texture.

5. Spread a layer of icing around the border of the serving board around the house to create a snowy look.

6. Use royal icing to stick sweets and chocolates onto the gingerbread house to decorate. Let your imagination go wild!

GLUTEN-FREE INDEX

THANK YOUS

Writing a book is an enjoyable and rewarding experience, but I have also found it challenging and have relied on many amazing people to help me through the process.

To Yasin, Maddie and Leon, you guys are superstars! I had so much fun working with you modelling pros. I hope you enjoyed the shoots and that you'll enjoy showing your friends that you're now famous in the bookshops!

To my auntie and the staff and students at Walkington Primary School. Thank you so much for welcoming me in to chat about baking and get busy in the kitchen. It was so much fun to feel your energy and learn about your passion in the kitchen.

To Susie, thank you for being a joy to work with and bringing such incredible energy to every photoshoot.

To Ali, Eve and Gordon, thanks for letting me clutter up your kitchen for two weeks so we could take the photos and make this book look awesome.

To Yellow Poppy Media and Black & White Publishing, thank you for your continued support and guidance in helping me get to the point of publishing my second book.

To my family, flatmates and friends, thank you for being such supportive ears listening to my ideas, expectations and concerns; for always being there and for sharing the fun and exciting moments of this baking journey with me. It wouldn't be anywhere near as fun without you.

Thanks to CALA homes for letting us use one of their Edinburgh show homes to take some photos.

Most importantly, thank you for coming to my baking party! I hope you have enjoyed the baking fun and will enjoy it for many years to come.

With best baking wishes,

Peter x

ABOUT PETER SAWKINS

Peter Sawkins, an accounting and finance student at the University of Edinburgh, is the youngest ever winner of the *Great British Bake Off*. A passionate baker since childhood, he credits the show as one of the reasons he embarked on his culinary journey. He is the author of *Peter Bakes*. *Peter's Baking Party* is his second book.

You can find Peter on Instagram and TikTok

@peter_bakes